Identity-Conscious Practice in Action

When teachers and leaders implement an identity-conscious practice, they can provide a more responsive and responsible learning environment. Unfortunately, avoiding the impact of identity can create problematic and oppressive conditions in schools.

So how do we lead with an identity-conscious lens? Award-winning author Liza Talusan provides real-world scenarios that educators can work through to apply an identity-conscious practice. Talusan helps educators grapple with three key questions: 1) How do I build knowledge about scenarios that involve identity? 2) How do my own thoughts, attitudes, behaviors, and beliefs contribute to inequitable conditions? 3) What actions can I implement in my classroom/meeting spaces to align with principles of equity and justice?

Readers explore these questions through case studies on race, class/socioeconomic status, religion/faith, disability, sexual orientation, gender, language, and age. With the book's numerous real-world examples, Talusan makes the concept of an identity-conscious practice more tangible, so you feel ready and empowered to implement it day-to-day in your own practice.

Liza Talusan, PhD, is an educator, speaker, leader, writer, coach, and parent. She has over 27 years of experience in PreK-20 education and is currently a faculty member in the College of Education and Human Development at the University of Massachusetts Boston. Her book, *The Identity-Conscious Educator: Building Habits and Skills for a More Inclusive School*, published by Solution Tree Press, is the 2023 Gold Medal Recipient of IPPY Awards.

Equity and Social Justice in Education Series

Paul C. Gorski, Series Editor

Routledge's Equity and Social Justice in Education series is a publishing home for books that apply critical and transformative equity and social justice theories to the work of on-the-ground educators. Books in the series describe meaningful solutions to the racism, white supremacy, economic injustice, sexism, heterosexism, transphobia, ableism, neoliberalism, and other oppressive conditions that pervade schools and school districts.

Embracing the Exceptions: Meeting the Needs of Neurodivergent Students of Color
JPB Gerald

Teaching Asian America in Elementary Schools
Noreen Naseem Rodriguez, Sohyun An, and Esther June Kim

Literacy for All: A Framework for Anti-Oppressive Teaching
Shawna Coppola

Social Studies for a Better World: An Anti-Oppressive Approach for Elementary Educators
Noreen Naseem Rodriguez and Katy Swalwell

Equity-Centered Trauma-Informed Education:
Alex Shevrin Venet

Learning and Teaching While White: Antiracist Strategies for School Communities
Jenna Chandler-Ward and Elizabeth Denevi

Public School Equity: Educational Leadership for Justice
Manya C. Whitaker

Identity-Conscious Practice in Action: Shaping Equitable Schools and Classrooms
Liza Talusan

Identity-Conscious Practice in Action

Shaping Equitable Schools and Classrooms

Liza Talusan

Routledge
Taylor & Francis Group
NEW YORK AND LONDON

Designed cover image: Getty Images

First published 2025
by Routledge
605 Third Avenue, New York, NY 10158

and by Routledge
4 Park Square, Milton Park, Abingdon, Oxon, OX14 4RN

Routledge is an imprint of the Taylor & Francis Group, an informa business

© 2025 Liza Talusan

The right of Liza Talusan to be identified as author of this work has been asserted in accordance with sections 77 and 78 of the Copyright, Designs and Patents Act 1988.

All rights reserved. No part of this book may be reprinted or reproduced or utilised in any form or by any electronic, mechanical, or other means, now known or hereafter invented, including photocopying and recording, or in any information storage or retrieval system, without permission in writing from the publishers.

Trademark notice: Product or corporate names may be trademarks or registered trademarks, and are used only for identification and explanation without intent to infringe.

ISBN: 978-1-032-82253-2 (pbk)
ISBN: 978-1-003-50848-9 (ebk)

DOI: 10.4324/9781003508489

Typeset in Palatino
by SPi Technologies India Pvt Ltd (Straive)

Dedicated to Emilia Bautista King, Yvonne Hill Adams, and the educators who have fought tirelessly for more equitable schools all the way to the end. Your stories ended too soon.

May your memory be a revolution.

Contents

Acknowledgements	x
Introduction	1
Outline of the Book	2
About the Author	3

PART I
An Introduction to an Identity-Conscious Practice — 5

1. Why Identity Matters in Schools — 7
2. The Foundations of an Identity-Conscious Practice — 9
3. Talking About Identity — 11
4. Examining Our Biases — 14
5. Beginning Your Identity-Conscious Practice — 17

PART II
Implementing an Identity-Conscious Practice — 19

6. Conflicts and Risks in an Identity-Conscious Practice — 21
   The Four I's — 24
7. Building Habits for an Identity-Conscious Practice: What Now? What Next? — 25
8. Guidelines for Reflection and Conversation — 27
   Critical Check Ins — 28
   Framework — 29
   Process — 29
   Peer Learning Groups — 30

PART III
Case Studies for Building an Identity-Conscious Practice — 33

9 Case Studies on Race — 35
Case 9.1: A Separate Affinity Group — 35
Case 9.2: The National Guard — 37
Case 9.3: A Place for Affinity — 39
Case 9.4: The Research Project — 41
Case 9.5: A Parent and Administrator Clash — 43

10 Case Studies on Socioeconomic Status — 46
Case 10.1: The Birthday Party — 46
Case 10.2: The Payscale — 48
Case 10.3: Difference Within — 50
Case 10.4: The Soup Kitchen — 51
Case 10.5: Art Supplies — 53

11 Case Studies on Religion/Faith — 56
Case 11.1: Song Choice and Choir — 56
Case 11.2: The Dining Hall — 58
Case 11.3: Read Aloud — 60
Case 11.4: World Events — 61
Case 11.5: Freedom to Express — 63

12 Case Studies on Disability — 65
Case 12.1: Recommendations for Employment — 65
Case 12.2: The Theater Performance — 67
Case 12.3: Neurodiversity and Staffing — 69
Case 12.4: The Assessment — 72
Case 12.5: Increased Stress — 73

13 Case Studies on Sexual Orientation — 76
Case 13.1: The First — 76
Case 13.2: Isolation — 78
Case 13.3: Everyone Says It — 80
Case 13.4: Health Education — 82
Case 13.5: Waiting to Respond — 84

14 Case Studies on Gender and Gender Identity — 86
Case 14.1: A Girl on the Team — 86
Case 14.2: Transitioning — 88
Case 14.3: Bathrooms and Access — 90

Case 14.4: The Group Project	92
Case 14.5: Disclosing Names and Pronouns	94

15 Case Studies on Language — **96**
Case 15.1: A Way to Connect	96
Case 15.2: The Email	98
Case 15.3: Must Speak English	99
Case 15.4: The Rubric	101
Case 15.5: The Competition	103

16 Case Studies on Age — **105**
Case 16.1: Set in My Ways	105
Case 16.2: A Word in the Meeting	107
Case 16.3: A New Assistant Director	109
Case 16.4: The Parent Group	111
Case 16.5: Someone to Mentor	113

17 Conclusion — **116**

References — **118**

Acknowledgements

This book is inspired by the many educators, teachers, school leaders, families, and those who are school adjacent who consistently work toward greater equity and inclusion. This work teeters between being energizing and exhausting. Thank you to those who continue to examine the systems that contribute to oppression and fight each day to dismantle barriers to thriving.

Thank you to my family – Jorge, Joli, Jay, and Evan - who live a life of identity-consciousness. Thank you for sharing your stories with me and for helping future teachers and school leaders learn from you.

Long before this book was written, my work has been inspired by Dr. Paul Gorski. In his work, writing, scholarship, and practice, I found a home for my voice. I shifted my own perspective from individual responsibility to an emphasis on systems and organizations. I stopped apologizing for my words and leaned into the idea that discomfort is part of the process. Thank you for being a co-conspirator in this educational space and for inviting this book into your home.

Thank you to my editing team of Divya Muthu (Project Manager) and Nick Brock (Copy-editor).

Thank you to the publishing, art, and graphics team.

Thank you to the Saturday Writing Team who shows up each week to disrupt academic norms of competition and, instead, supports each other in our writing processes. Thank you for holding me accountable to this book and to writing through joy.

Thank you to Lisa O'Donnell who keeps me focused, organized, and employed. Your friendship and your partnership mean so much to me.

Thank you to my parents, Eduardo and Araceli Talusan, who immigrated to this country and risked so much so that my siblings and I could pursue our dreams of being educators, writers, scholars, and providers. Thank you to Mary, Grace, Paul, and Jonathan for being my first friends and my greatest role models.

And thank you to the educators, teachers, and school leaders who are on the frontlines of these case studies every single day. Thank you to John Sharon, Michelle Holmes, Priscilla Morales, current and former students, and countless others who provided some ideas for case studies in this book.

Introduction

Identity informs how we act, interact, and how we see the world around us.

(Talusan, 2022)

During the winter of 2019–2020, I wrote a book called *The Identity-Conscious Educator: Building Habits and Skills for More Inclusive Schools*. Teachers and school leaders adopted the text in their professional development practices, all-school reads, and leadership discussions. As they made their way through the book, readers built knowledge about key aspects of identity, engaged in reflection about their own identities, and identified action plans for how they wanted to shape a more inclusive school. They formed peer learning communities and created action plans that focused on naming, owning, and interrupting oppressive conditions in schools.

While *The Identity-Conscious Educator* offered a helpful framework for building more inclusive schools, many readers wanted further assistance in applying an identity-conscious framework to decision-making. They wanted an opportunity to discuss with their colleagues how decisions are made and how identity informed and impacted those decisions. They wanted scenarios to talk through with their teams as they created more equitable outcomes in their classrooms and school communities. These requests led to the book you have today: *Identity-Conscious Practice in Action: Shaping Equitable Schools and Classrooms*. Taken together, these two texts help you build an identity-conscious practice and apply it to every day decisions.

DOI: 10.4324/9781003508489-1

The pace of school moves very quickly and often requires teachers and school leaders to make decisions based on their previous experiences. What if those previous experiences did not take into account the impact of identity? How might past behavior predict future decisions? In this book, I invite you to slow down. I invite you to examine a situation and ask big questions about how identity is showing up. I invite you to play with the process of decision-making by integrating aspects of identity into the process. I invite you to examine scenarios, think critically about identity, and have your future decision-making be identity-conscious.

The book is driven by three (3) key essential questions:

1. How do I build knowledge about scenarios that involve identity?
2. How do I, as a teacher or leader, uphold or perpetuate problematic thoughts, attitudes, behaviors, and beliefs that may be contributing to oppressive conditions?
3. What actions do I need to implement in my classroom/meeting spaces to align with principles of equity and justice?

By using the method of case studies as a way to engage these questions, readers can examine how identity informs and impacts their behaviors and beliefs through practical examples. The goal is not to "solve the problem"; rather, it is to engage in a thoughtful process that may reveal there are multiple solutions to any one problem or challenge. Engaging in an identity-conscious practice will uncover that issues are more complicated and complex than they initially seem. By utilizing an identity-conscious practice in case studies, the reader has the opportunity to think deeply about the role of identity and to develop a more inclusive and equitable response.

Outline of the Book

The book is presented in three distinct and related parts. In Part I, the reader is given an introduction to an identity-conscious practice where we explore why identity matters in schools. We will examine the existing deficits in our understanding of identity in schools and begin to develop foundations of an identity-conscious practice.

In Part II, we will take the foundational scholarship and begin the process of implementing an identity-conscious practice. The reader will examine the conflicts and risks of engaging in an identity-conscious practice and develop an action plan for the teaching, learning, and learning environment. In this process, the reader will engage with questions that will help build their own identity-conscious practice.

In Part III, we will take the key components of Parts I and II and apply them to case studies. The case studies are organized by themes. At the end of each case study, key questions are presented to the reader to encourage thinking through the case studies from an identity-conscious lens.

Classroom teachers will find this text helpful as they develop the habits and skills of engaging in an identity-conscious practice in their teaching, leading, learning, grading, evaluation, and relationship building. School leaders will find this text helpful to run table-top exercises that address existing challenges within the school setting and to proactively set up policies, practices, programs, and procedures that support a more inclusive and equitable environment. Parents, caregivers, and communities that are education-adjacent will find these case studies helpful in examining the larger context of identity and education.

In this book, all names (e.g., individuals, schools, and districts) are entirely made up. Any resemblance to existing individuals, schools, districts, or situations are purely coincidental.

About the Author

Dr. Liza (LIE-zuh) Talusan (taLOOS-ahn) is an educator, speaker, leader, writer, coach, and parent. With over 27 years of experience in PreK-20 education, Liza is an engaging facilitator in conversations about diversity, anti-racism, bias, privilege, and power and creates environments that allow for people to discuss these difficult topics openly.

Liza is the recipient of numerous awards, including "Best 40 Under 40"; NASPA Region I Mid-Level Professional Award; NASPA APIKC VIP Award; Asian Women for Health's Peer Leader Award; Promise in Action Mentoring Nominee; Network for Equity, Excellence in Education Award; the REAPA (AERA) Dissertation of the Year Award; the Harriet Buescher Lawrence Prize from Connecticut College; the Early Career Award (REAPA); the YMCA Leadership Award; the 2024 NAACP Brockton Phenomenal Women Award; and a number of institutional grants.

She earned her Bachelor degree from Connecticut College; Masters of Arts from New York University; Ph.D. from University of Massachusetts Boston; Certificate in Human Resources; and her PCC Coaching Credentials from the Institute for Professional Excellence in Coaching. Liza is currently a faculty member in the College of Education and Human Development at the

University of Massachusetts Boston where she teaches courses on leadership and anti-racism in education.

Liza has been a guest on a number of podcasts focused on educational equity and is the new co-host for the podcast Teaching While white. Liza's book, *The Identity-Conscious Educator: Building Habits and Skills for More Inclusive Schools* with Jenna Chandler-Ward and Elizabeth Denevi, published by Solution Tree Press, is the 2023 Gold Medal Recipient of IPPY Awards.

Part I
An Introduction to an Identity-Conscious Practice

1

Why Identity Matters in Schools

Chapter at a Glance

This chapter explores why identity talk supports a more creative, innovative, and engaging classroom/learning environment.

One does not need to go too far to find someone who believes that talking about issues of identity – or diversity, equity, and inclusion – are "divisive." People say, "Talking about racism makes people feel bad" or "Children are too young to know about sexual orientation" or "Talking about issues of class makes people feel guilty." Comments like these shut down conversations. But building healthy habits and skills for productive conversations can be meaningful. When we focus on building healthy habits and skills for working across differences, we build stronger communities.

Where does identity fall in these discussions? Identity is a part of everything that we do, even if we have not unmasked or revealed its impact. An identity-conscious approach is the process of realizing that who we are informs and impacts how we act, interact, and see the world around us. If that approach is true, then nothing in our lives is identity-neutral. How we teach, advise, learn, parent, mentor, grade, discipline, publish, research, and fundraise, to name a few, is all informed and impacted by identity.

Because talking about identity requires healthy habits and skills for inclusive relationships, conversations, and opportunities, it is important to integrate conversations about identity in the work of our schools. After all, math, language, history, literature, art, music, and even physical education classes are not identity-neutral. Our identities as teachers inform and impact what types of books we choose, articles we read, activities we facilitate, and papers that we grade. The identities of our students are impacted by the decisions that we make each day, and these choices can affirm/validate or diminish/make invisible the lives of our students.

Adults in schools play a key role in the decision-making processes. Too often, decisions are made without taking into account how identity shows up. Without considering the role of identity, our decisions result in inequitable and narrow solutions. What would it mean if we had the opportunity to examine issues through an identity-conscious lens? Our decisions would be more inclusive, would be more reflective of our communities, and would be centered on impact. The case studies in this book provide opportunities for us to build these habits and skills through a mix of situations that involve multiple constituents (e.g., teachers, leaders, parent councils, boards) and identity based scenarios.

2

The Foundations of an Identity-Conscious Practice

Chapter at a Glance

This chapter explores the concept of an identity-conscious practice – the process of realizing that who we are informs and impacts how we act, interact, and see the world around us.

An identity-conscious practice begins with understanding who we are. For example, I identify as an Asian American woman, a mother, a wife, a sister, and a daughter. I identify as a scholar, practitioner, educator. I identify as an athlete, as able-bodied, and as plus-sized. I identify as a child and sister of those formerly undocumented; as a mother to multiracial activists; as a learner.

These identities shape how I move through the world, what I pay attention to, and what I tend to privilege in my schedule. When I look at my life, my teaching, my syllabus, and the decisions I make, they are largely influenced by the identities I wrote above. These identities that I hold sometimes impact me negatively and sometimes impact me positively. For example, I think about my identity as an athlete – I carve out significant time during my week to train (i.e., distance running, martial arts, stretching, physical therapy) and that impacts decisions I make related to my work. My identity as a woman of color informs the issues I pay attention to and where I spend my hours in advocacy.

While I am aware of the identities that I hold, an identity-conscious practice also means knowing which identities I do not have closeness or proximity to. While I identify as Asian American, married to an Afro-Puerto Rican man, and mother to multiracial children, I do not have proximity to other racial identities such as Native and Indigenous communities. My life of relative privilege means that I do not have closeness or proximity to those who experience homelessness or those who may be food-insecure. Having been raised by my biological parents means that I do not have proximity to experiences with adoption or fostering or being raised by extended family members. Because of who I am and what I have experienced, I have particular blank spots to understanding other life experiences.

These blank spots become increasingly evident when I am faced with decision-making. As a former school administrator, I was often put in the position of making decisions about particular communities or groups of people. And, too often, I was given the power to make decisions that would impact people who come from experiences I would never know or understand. An identity-conscious practice requires me to build an awareness of identities and experiences that are close to me; those that are known to me but not as familiar; and those that are unfamiliar.

As a researcher, I am guided by the motto "Never about us without us." Essentially, when making decisions, are those who are most impacted included in the decision-making process? Or, are people who have no closeness, knowledge, or proximity to an experience making these decisions? Having spent over two decades in schools, I can confidently tell you that, far too often, school leaders are making decisions about situations or experiences that they do not have closeness to. These decisions, because they are not rooted in community, can be oppressive or uphold oppressive actions.

"We keep doing the same thing and expecting different results." How often have you found yourself in this situation? Whether it is work, school, family, relationships, or behaviors, we sometimes get in patterns that are unproductive. Yet, we repeat these patterns because we believe that maybe this time will be different. Well, the time is now to do something different to achieve different results. Building an identity-conscious practice – a process that can support us in making more responsible and responsive decisions – may just be that pathway.

3

Talking About Identity

Chapter at a Glance

Not everyone has learned the habits and skills for recognizing identity, the impact of identity, and one's role in identity work. This chapter provides the reader with a few frameworks for how to engage in this work productively.

On MLK Day, my family and I engaged in a local volunteer event. We were tasked with packing meals for students to bring home on the weekends when free lunch was not available at school. Because of this particular day, a friend of mine asked me why I focused so much on issues of race. She said, "I grew up with the belief that we just have to see people as people. And, as a Christian, I believe that God's message is for me to treat everyone as human. I do believe racism exists and I know that there are structures that have made things unequal. But, I don't see race. I treat everyone the same." I understood this sentiment. In particular, I know this comes up during MLK weekend when people bring up Dr. King's misquoted phrase of "content of character and not color of skin."

"Sure," I replied. "And I'm glad you acknowledge that racism is real and baked into our laws, policies, and traditions. I, too, want to live in a world where we can all just be people and treated without our identifiers serving as barriers to access and success." As we continued our conversation, I noticed that the other participants at the event were starting to leave. This conversation was going to take a while, so I explained to my friend, who identifies as white, that my son and I should leave soon because we don't want to be the last ones in the building. "Why?" she asked. "Well," I replied, "My son is male, tall, and has dark brown skin and big curly hair. If he wanders this area alone, someone is likely to call and say that a 'dark skin man' was seen leaving a closed building. While you know my son to be sweet, kind, friendly, goofy, and adorable, not everyone will see him that way. It is safer if we leave with you." She replied, "I know you're right. I just want to believe that it doesn't happen."

Sometimes people confuse "noticing race" with "discriminating on the basis of race." While they can be connected, noticing identity does not equal discrimination. Ignoring race does not cure racism. Instead, we need to be able to notice it, name when negative associations come to mind, and interrupt behaviors that lead to discrimination. The fact that my friend is a good person who is caring and kind does not negate that race matters. Raising her identity-consciousness can help her see how our awareness can help us be better friends, allies, and advocates in particular situations.

One activity that has helped me to understand the impact of identity-consciousness is proximity. Proximity mapping helps us to identify where we feel close or connected; which identities are important to us but are not central to our experiences; and which identities we are unfamiliar with or have a great deal of distance to.

Step 1: Make a list of different categories of identities. This could include race, class, gender, disability, religion, age, etc.

(a) Closest distance; most important to who I am; most familiar to me
(b) Important to me but some distance (not my own)
(c) Very distant from my own experience, unfamiliar to me

Step 2: Within each category, identify if there are more nuances that you may want to be more specific. For example, in the category RACE, I feel closest to the identity of Asian American (a); my family identifies as Afro-Latinx and as multiracial, so I'd mark a (b). I do not experience closeness to communities that identify as Native American (c) or white (c).

Step 3: To extend this experience, draw out a visual map. Place a representation of yourself on the page, and then begin to map out areas (a), (b), and (c) to visually demonstrate location and proximity.

Once we have identified how close or far we are to certain identities, we can begin to ask ourselves, "How does proximity inform and impact the work that I do?" That work can include our teaching, leading, learning, advising, coaching, collaborating, and decision-making. Without proximity mapping, we might rush to make decisions without considering different identities and experiences. You will be using this proximity map as you work through the case studies in this book to highlight how your own identities might inform and impact your decision-making.

4

Examining Our Biases

Chapter at a Glance

Biases shape our attitudes, thoughts, behaviors, and beliefs. This chapter guides the reader to explore different biases they may have and how those biases inform and impact an identity-conscious practice.

An identity-conscious lens takes practice. As teachers and school leaders, we are often relying on our view of the world or past experiences to shape how we respond. While this may have served us well, we need to constantly interrogate our own worldviews and responses. Biases are how we see the world and how we make decisions. Sometimes, our biases benefit us. Sometimes, our biases harm others.

Rudine Sims Bishop (1990) highlights how important it is for us to have windows and mirrors in our world. It is important for us to see ourselves reflected in curriculum, teaching, learning, and in stories. Similarly, it is important for us to learn about others and different experiences through these same pathways. But these windows and mirrors result in different reactions. When we see mirrors – reflections of ourselves – we tend to feel connected, familiar, and understood. When we encounter windows – experiences that are different from ours – we may express curiosity and wonder or even uncertainty and hesitation. A similar concept exists in the language of bias.

Psychologists who study bias have noted many different types of biases that exist. Specifically for an identity-conscious practice, *attentional bias* – the tendency to focus on certain elements while ignoring others – is a key process for examining the world (Cherry, 2024). *Confirmation bias* is the tendency to search for information that supports a belief while ignoring information that contradicts it (Myers and DeWall, 2015). When we seek information that only supports our identity lens, we leave out other types of identities and experiences. *Ingroup bias* is a tendency to choose those who are similar to you over those who are not. Researchers have found that children as young as three years old already display preferences for ingroup companions (Hailey & Olson, 2013).

In order for us to address the impact of bias, we can learn how to reduce, eliminate, or counteract the processes that contribute to the tendencies in attentional bias, confirmation bias, and ingroup bias. By engaging in an identity-conscious practice, an individual can begin to understand where they tend to pay most attention and where they identify others as outgroup or different from their experiences. While it is not possible to always move outgroup members to the ingroup, our awareness of this can shape more responsible decision-making. For example, think about your own leadership or teaching team. How many times have you made decisions about a community, population, or individual without anyone from those groups representing a voice? I have been at tables where we have made decisions about people who are food-insecure; where we have made decisions about public transportation; where we have made decisions about keeping residence halls open for international students. Yet, in each of those scenarios, none of the people at the table would have been impacted by those decisions. Our administrative team – the decision-makers – were not proximate to those experiences. How often are decisions made at the senior level without any input of those most affected?

Biases do not just occur randomly, however. They are learned through passive or active teaching. They are reinforced whenever we see examples of our biases in the world. And they are perpetuated by us and passed along to others. How has this happened? It happens through influences. Our thoughts, attitudes, behaviors, and beliefs are shaped by the world around us. As an exercise, I would like for you to pick an identity category (e.g., race, class, gender, sexual orientation, disability, religion) and answer the questions below.

How have your thoughts, attitudes, behaviors, and beliefs about _____ (the category you selected) been informed and impacted by _____(see below)

- ◆ How you were raised
- ◆ What you were taught formally in school
- ◆ What you were taught informally
- ◆ Who you knew

- What your family told you
- What your culture encouraged
- What you believed
- What you experienced
- What you did not experience
- How you have been treated

For me, I was raised Catholic in a town that had many other Catholics (two Catholic churches, in fact!). I know that I have particular *thoughts, attitudes, behaviors, and beliefs about religion* that have been informed and impacted by *who I knew* (mostly Catholics) and who I didn't know (almost every other religious group). The first time I met someone who was Hindu was my second year in college. To this date, I have never been inside a synagogue for service. I have only met a few Buddhists. The first time I met someone who was Bahá'í, I was twenty-four years old. It is accurate to say that my limited exposure to people other than Catholics shaped my experiences.

Through these influencers, we developed biases. We developed a way that we see the world and those around us. These messages can also change over the course of your life. For example, go back into the list and mark any of the items that have changed for you. For example, I held certain thoughts, attitudes, behaviors, and beliefs about the LGBTQ+ community from my upbringing in the Catholic church, from my religious family members, from the lack of role models in my own life, from the invisibility of LGBTQ+ people in my formal curriculum, and for the ways that I heard friends exclude LGBTQ+ people. Today, as an adult who is constantly working on dismantling biases in my life, I can confidently say that I do not hold those same thoughts, attitudes, behaviors, and beliefs that were a part of my upbringing. But it would be dishonest of me to believe that those early messages had no impact. Rather, I find myself having quick reactions rooted in those early influences. My job is to slow that response down and reevaluate why I felt that way. Each time that I practice naming, owning, and interrupting my early messages, I am building an identity-conscious practice. As I continue to learn and grow, I know that my decision-making is informed and impacted by these new messages of greater representation and inclusion of LGBTQ+ issues, communities, and people. But, if not for that opportunity to slow down and address my biases, I might simply continue to perpetuate harm.

As teachers and school leaders, we have a responsibility to provide a safe, inclusive, and critical environment for our students to learn and grow. The work begins with us — the decision-makers, the keepers of power in these schools, and those who shape the environment. When we create greater inclusion and equity in our schools, we have a greater chance of shaping actual belonging.

5

Beginning Your Identity-Conscious Practice

Chapter at a Glance

In this chapter, the reader is encouraged to engage in practice and reflection as opposed to always reacting. This chapter serves as a touchpoint for the work the reader will do in Parts II and III.

Growing up, I was not the best athlete. I tried out for multiple sports and never made it past tryouts or was put on a team specially created for those who needed a little more help. After realizing team sports was maybe not my strength, I enrolled in martial arts at the age of sixteen. Martial arts was more focused on the individual, and it seemed like a good way to stay in shape and learn some important skills. As my priorities changed, I had to let go of karate training: college, graduate school, starting my family, moving, changing jobs. In 2013, I signed my two children up for karate classes. I sat in the audience wishing I could do what they were doing. With some gentle persuading, I eventually signed up for my first karate class as an adult in 2017.

While some might believe that karate is all about kicking and punching, karate actually taught me about patience and practice. In order to master certain moves, forms, defenses, and weapons, we learn how to do them very slowly. We repeat a small set of moves week after week. Only after we have demonstrated an understanding of those moves are we allowed to move on to the next. We slow down to get better. We slow down because repetition builds the muscle memory needed if and when danger occurs.

Practice and patience is key to this book. In an emergency situation at school or in a classroom, you need to react *quickly*. But, in order to react *productively*, you actually need to slow everything down in practice sessions.

Building an identity-conscious practice requires us to engage in the discipline of slowing down. We slow down, read case studies, and have conversations with each other so that if and when the time comes when we need to be reactive, we have already built the muscle memory of working from an identity-conscious framework. As you read this book, you may need to fight the urge to "solve the problem of the case." While a solution to the problem is one outcome, the goal of the work is to be thoughtful, to be reflective, and to implement an identity-conscious practice.

As you build the habits and skills of seeing the world around you through an identity-conscious lens, you begin to notice that there are behaviors, decisions, and actions that simply dismiss identity. You will begin to notice the shallowness of decisions that could be made more robust if identity were considered in the process. You will begin to see how certain identities and experiences are centered and privileged in your teaching and leading.

Reading these case studies from an identity-conscious lens requires you to listen to the stories of others and how their identities have shaped their views. Consider how these different approaches might impact a situation, a decision, and an outcome. This book is not prompting you to find the right answer. Instead, an identity-conscious practice requires you to constantly examine the role of identity in the world around us.

Part II
Implementing an Identity-Conscious Practice

6

Conflicts and Risks in an Identity-Conscious Practice

Chapter at a Glance

Equity and justice work is conflict work. This work requires people to push against existing systems that have been historically and currently oppressive. Therefore, readers who engage in building an identity-conscious practice should also think about their own thresholds for conflicts and risk. This chapter guides the reader to identify what this means at the individual level, interpersonal level, institutional level, and ideological level.

For the past few years, issues of racial justice were a central dialogue in the nation sparked by the killing of George Floyd in 2020 and a series of violent attacks that followed. Amid these events was emerging violence against Asian and Asian Americans who were being blamed for the COVID-19 pandemic; ongoing oppression against Latinx communities, particularly at the southern border; and the rising impact of lack of access to resources in Native and Indigenous communities. Many schools and organizations started addressing issues of racism in their own practices. While this movement prompted many schools to address and reduce racism in schools, an opposing movement influenced by political ideology began their attack on anything affiliated with "DEI" or diversity, equity, and inclusion. Theoretical frameworks that were once reserved for academic inquiry, such as Critical Race Theory, were intentionally misused and misapplied in common practice. And parents and caregivers, fearful that their children would be uncomfortable learning the truths

DOI: 10.4324/9781003508489-9

about American history, organized book bans and ended funding that provided a more diverse and truthful perspective.

What was driving some of these behaviors? One of these drivers is values. Values tend to drive our behaviors. When we value something, we act in ways that bring us closer to what we value. Additionally, we fight for things that we value so they will not be taken away from us. In the past few years, as social issues have escalated into the halls of Congress and most recently to the Supreme Court, the values of those who hold positional power drive their behaviors that influence our communities. One common phrase I hear people say when we are talking about anti-racism work is "reverse racism." They believe that providing greater equity – conditions that might require them to give something up – is just being "racist in reverse." Of course, I do not agree with this. I usually follow up with, "So you don't like or trust DEI work. What is it that you value?" They have responded, "We value truth. We value freedom. We value schools where kids feel comfortable and aren't made to feel guilty about who they are." My response is always, "I value the same thing."

So, why does this reaction get such a response? The conflict comes when I highlight that we value the same things – they just do not value it for everyone. They value those things for themselves. There is an implied word that is missing in their response: our. "We value (our) freedom. We value schools where (our) kids feel comfortable and aren't made to feel guilty about who they are." However, for many children of color, they have been educated in systems that were not telling the truth about enslavement or colonization. Our schools were not always drawing attention to who had to pay the price in order for freedom to be free in this country. Our schools have not always been places where children of color feel comfortable or who aren't made to feel guilty for who they are.

To engage in dialogues like this, however, invites conflict and risk. We have become a community of binaries and ultimatums. We have become a community of canceling each other and shaming each other. What would happen if we, instead, were a community that held each other accountable? What would happen if we were accountable to all students, families, and faculty? What would happen if we were held accountable to make sure that the values of truth, freedom, and safety were for all? What would be different about our schools? What kinds of risks would we need to take to make sure that happened?

Not everyone can take the same risks when it comes to equity and justice. For example, as a cisgender woman and heterosexual, I have held roles where my work included supporting LGBTQ+ students and families. A group of LGBTQ+ families wanted to participate in a PRIDE parade as a school and asked me to organize this first-time event. While the school stated it was progressive and liberal, it was clear that there were some families who did not support the school's participation at the event. There was conflict and risk. I knew that my identities as heterosexual and cisgender woman allowed me to advocate for participating in the parade. I knew that my job included supporting LGBTQ+ families. And I knew that I had colleagues who would also speak up. The risk for me and my identities was low even though some parents created conflict.

There are also times when I was not able to engage as fully in the conflict and risk that is required of justice work. In 2021, the general public began to hear a term that had been used for decades in academia: Critical Race Theory. Some people misused and weaponized to create fear in the general public. People who had never heard of this academic framework were suddenly opposed to it and seeking out any educators who used the letters C-R-T. During this time, one of my workshops that included issues of race was leaked to the news. A slide was taken out of context, shared on social media, and this brought a great deal of unwanted attention to me. Headlines were used for clickbait but none of it was relevant to the actual dialogue we had in the workshop. Soon after this was leaked, I received emails using disparaging slurs about my ethnicity, race, and gender. Emails about my intentions, how my very presence was offensive, and that I should not be teaching filled my inbox. I do not like admitting this, but the pushback on me was successful. For months, I did not give public workshops about race and racism. I did not post as openly as I used to do. I did not let people record my workshops, and I no longer shared any of my slides. I put in place what I could to protect myself and my family.

During that time, I had watched my friends and people I admire continue on with their work. They were courageously putting their voices out into the world and calling out those who harmed them. They were not hiding and not staying silent. I felt immense guilt that I was not doing the same. I felt shame for letting those emails and tweets get to me. I felt discouraged that I might never do this work publicly again. For a brief moment in time, this had a chilling effect on me.

Things have changed in my professional life. I am back in the public eye and doing workshops for schools and organizations. But, I find myself hesitant when I am asked to do certain types of workshops. In reflection, going through these experiences required me to lean into my identity-conscious practice. What was it about my identities and experiences that informed and impacted my response to this attention? How did my identities as a mother, as a wife, as a daughter, and as a sister inform and impact my willingness to take risks? How did my identities as a scholar, a writer, and a teacher inform and impact those risks? How did my identities as a business owner, as a financial provider for my family inform and impact those risks?

Engaging in my own identity-conscious practice allowed me to make sense – or at least gain clarity – into the decisions that I made. Engaging in an identity-conscious practice also helped me – or at least tried to help me – make sense of the vitriol and anger that was sent to me by strangers. While they were mostly anonymous or penned under false names, I had to believe that these people felt too far from these issues to understand what I was saying. It reminded me that other people's biases were shaped by what they learned, what they were hearing, and what they were believing.

The Four I's

In identity-conscious work, I have found that the framework of the Four I's – *ideological, institutional, interpersonal, and individual* – has helped me locate where risk and conflict might live in any situation. At the *ideological level*, we examine conflict and risk in people's belief systems and their values. For example, "What is it that we believe about education?" or "What is it that we believe about hiring practices?" At the *institutional level*, we examine conflict and risk at the organizational level through how those ideologies are upheld. For example, "What policies do we put in place that support our beliefs about hiring?" or "How does our belief about education show up in our student and faculty handbook?" At the *interpersonal level*, we examine the impact of what we believe and what we uphold through the relationships and interactions that exist. For example, "We believe that candidates from Ivy League Schools are the most qualified to work here, so at job fairs we will likely be more aggressive and outgoing with those candidates" or "Education should be about projects and group learning, therefore most of your assignments require you to be in groups." Finally, at the *individual level*, we examine conflicts and risks at the personal level. For example, "I shouldn't bother applying to that school because I know they only take Ivy League grads" or "I'm often picked last in group projects, and that's the only thing my teachers assign."

Taken together, an identity-conscious practice and the Four I's help us to locate where our biases might exist and how our decisions impact others. Conflict and risk exist at different levels. Building an identity-conscious practice helps us see where our own risks and conflicts live, and where we might need to be aware of risks and conflicts for others.

7

Building Habits for an Identity-Conscious Practice

What Now? What Next?

> **Chapter at a Glance**
>
> While this book focuses on skill building for how to name, own, and interrupt problematic attitudes, thoughts, and behaviors related to identity in schools, this section guides the reader to build explicit habits – ongoing commitments and accountability – by slowing down.

For many years, I served as a student affairs administrator at the college level. Part of the training that goes into this position often involves various internships, assistantships, and entry-level positions where I was on-call to respond to emergency situations on campus. I had to be quick on my feet to solve issues related to fire drills, emergency situations (e.g., students being transported to the hospital, phone calls to parents and caregivers, situations of bias) where there was little time to think. In those situations, reaction time was everything.

It is true that school leaders and teachers often have to react quickly. What does an identity-conscious practice have to do with reaction time? An identity-conscious practice requires us to slow down, to consider multiple perspectives, and then respond. You may be saying, "But, Liza, sometimes you have to make a split second decision in an emergency." Yes, true. That is the performance; engaging in these case studies in the practice. We practice so that we can perform well.

This book is designed to have you slow down, consider the impact of identity, and share your process with others. As you proceed to the case studies in this book, you may find the urge to solve the problems. Use this opportunity to slow down, read for nuances in these situations, and apply an identity-conscious lens. Doing so helps us to build that muscle memory. Will it always be this slow? No. As teachers and school leaders, crises do not slow down just because we want them to. But, the work you will do in this book will help you to consider identity through practice. By practicing the questions and scenarios in this book, you will learn to react to situations in a more inclusive and equitable way.

8

Guidelines for Reflection and Conversation

Chapter at a Glance

This chapter provides practical suggestions for working through the identity-conscious framework. Readers are introduced to Critical Check Ins, Name it/Own it/Interrupt it/Take responsibility, and helpful guidelines for a productive discussion.

Case studies are a helpful way of guiding a reader through a process of making equitable, well-thought-out, and practical decisions. This chapter provides evidence for why and how case studies can be used as well as the suggested processes for using case studies in peer learning communities.

Many teachers and school leaders have developed skills for noticing problems and offering quick solutions:

- A teacher sees an argument brewing in the back corner of the classroom. The teacher quickly calls the names of the people in the group and asks, "What's going on back there?" The teacher might tell the students to either get back to work or find a new activity.
- A teacher sees a child upset at their desk. The teacher quietly approaches the student, leans over the desk and whispers, "You okay? What happened?"
- A school leader sees a child wandering in the hallway when they should be in class and yells out, "Hey there! Get back to class. Let's go!"

DOI: 10.4324/9781003508489-11

While all of these actions quickly address an issue, there is a layer that is missing: the role of identity. For example, data has demonstrated that students of color are often disciplined at higher rates than white students. Related to gender, disruptive behavior in boys is often treated as normal, but the same behavior in girls is treated as problematic or manipulative (National Women's Law Center, & the Education Trust, n.d.). Related to mental health, children are often treated as if they are purposefully deviating from acceptable behavior rather than being treated with compassion and understanding for their social and emotional needs. In each of these examples, the role of identity and identity-consciousness can inform and impact how a teacher or school leader interprets, addresses, and follows up with the situation. Unless we center the impact of identity, we continue to perpetuate conditions that uphold an identity-avoidant answer. In the following chapters, the use of case studies allows the reader to start with the role of identity.

Critical Check Ins

Knowing that identity informs and impacts how one acts, interacts, and sees the world around them, it is important for the reader to prepare. Our responses to particular case studies may tap into an emotional response – sometimes these emotional responses can be positive and helpful while at other times an emotional response can be damaging or interfere with a situation. It is important, particularly in a process like case studies, to build the habits and skills for noticing our own emotions.

To do this, a process of Critical Check Ins is a helpful way to identify one's readiness to respond. Before each case study, build the habits of asking yourself the following questions:

1. On a scale of 1 (not very) to 10 (very), how **prepared** do you feel to engage in the case study process?
2. On a scale of 1 (not very) to 10 (very), how **familiar** are you with the topic that this case study addresses (e.g., race, class, gender, sexual orientation)?
3. On a scale of 1 (not very) to 10 (very), how **often** have you encountered situations related to the topic of this case study (e.g., race, class, gender, sexual orientation)?
4. On a scale of 1 (not very) to 10 (very), how **connected** do you feel to the topic of this case study?
5. On a scale of 1 (not very) to 10 (very), how **comfortable** are you talking about the kinds of issues that this case study addresses?

Critical Check Ins is a helpful habit to build as it brings awareness to your own readiness, feelings about the topic, and preparedness to engage in the work. When done in a larger group conversation, Critical Check Ins also helps to build some knowledge about the group process — where might there be strengths in the group related to this topic? Where might there be some gaps in preparedness to address the situations in the chapter? Asking these scaling questions helps to build awareness of identity and our responses to the case studies, and prepares us to think about possible action items rooted in our own experiences.

Framework

When reading, reflecting, and acting upon the situations in the case study, it is important to use a framework for examining the components within the sample. One helpful framework that utilizes an identity-conscious practice is called "Name It, Own It, Interrupt It, Take Responsibility."

Framework	Situation	Notes
Name it	What issues of identity may be showing up in this scenario?	
Own it	Why am I noticing those issues of identity? How am I feeling as I read/experience this scenario?	
Interrupt it	What actions, rooted in an identity-conscious practice, would be helpful to interrupt these behaviors?	
Take Responsibility	What follow up is necessary? What is my role in this follow up?	

Process

While it is tempting to engage in old behaviors of rushing to a solution, an identity-conscious case study approach requires the reader to slow down, engage in reflection, and develop thoughtful answers to each situation. It is important to remember that generating multiple responses can be a helpful way to engage in an identity-conscious practice, one that widens the lens of opportunity, of interpretation, and of solution generation.

In order to do this, it is recommended that the reader follow a process for engaging in these case studies:

1. Conduct Critical Check In prior to reading the case study
2. Read the case study and highlight any relevant information for you
3. Use the Name it, Own it, Interrupt it, Take Responsibility Framework for an identity-conscious practice
4. Check in using reflection questions about your own identity-conscious practice
5. Create a space for different approaches to the scenarios

As a reminder, situations often include complex components that require a contextual approach. The goal for these case studies is not to come up with the "right answer" but rather to identify a process that centers identity and engages critical thinking.

Peer Learning Groups

A healthy way of building the habits and skills of your community is to engage in dialogue in peer learning communities. These communities should be small enough for everyone to be able to participate. I recommend groups of 5–7 people. You might choose to have the groups stay together the entire academic year or mix them up. You might choose to have the groups separated by departments or have a diversity of roles in a group. Your decisions are largely informed by the dynamic of your community, the level of trust that exists, and the purpose of the peer learning communities. As you create these groups, there are a few other suggestions that I might offer:

- **Be mindful of the identities of people in the group**. While it might not always be possible, having someone be the "only" in the group can be challenging. For example, having only one person of color in a group might create conditions of isolation. Try to create opportunities for people to share at least one identity with others in the group.
- **Manage expectations**. There is a limited amount of time in your day. These cases can be complicated and the process might need more than twenty minutes in your staff meeting. As stated, the goal is not to solve the case studies. The goal is to engage in a process where thinking about identity is embedded in decision-making. Create time where people can slow down.

- **Be willing to make mistakes, but be responsible for them**. In order to learn, grow, and change, we must also be willing to make mistakes. Give people grace as they take risks in this learning process. We must create conditions where it is okay to fail. At the same time, our own ignorance is not an excuse. We must take responsibility for when we have hurt someone or been limited in our thinking. Creating conditions for learning requires both a willingness to take risks and to be responsible for them.
- **Create conditions for learning**. This book is designed to help build the habits and skills of implementing an identity-conscious practice. Because of that approach, it is important to center the practice of learning in your peer groups. What do people need in order to learn? What do people need in order to grow? These might be helpful questions to ask the group.
- **Provide continuity**. Many people will use this book during their own reflections or in small groups (e.g., classrooms, peer learning communities, faculty development). While they might be in dialogues for that duration of time, it is important to come up with action items for how this work can carry beyond the meeting. Ask your group, "What did we learn from this discussion? How might this discussion inform and impact decisions outside of this setting?"
- **Stay ready. Be humble**. Even if you have been doing identity work your entire career, there are still things you can learn. Be ready to share your wisdom and expertise with others. But be open to learning a new idea, perspective, and approach that you might not have considered. It takes humility to engage in the learning process.

Part III
Case Studies for Building an Identity-Conscious Practice

9

Case Studies on Race

Chapter at a Glance

This chapter presents five case studies related to race. Readers are encouraged to review the case study, engage in reflective practice using the guided questions provided, and participate in peer learning communities for dialogue. The goal is not to solve the case but rather practice slowing down, using an identity-conscious lens, and creating action for future use.

Case 9.1: A Separate Affinity Group

Ms. Cho is an Asian American woman who serves as a middle school English teacher and part-time Coordinator of Diversity and Inclusion at her school. The middle school Black Affinity Group is one of the strongest groups in terms of numbers and participation and is often led by the 8th grade members of the group. Ms. Cho has noted that a small group of 7th grade girls have had a tough time connecting in the affinity group. They identify as more introverted than the larger group.

The four 7th grade girls have asked if Ms. Cho would be willing to host a separate affinity group session. The 7th graders have enjoyed eating lunch together, and asked Ms. Cho if they could meet up during a few lunch sessions as their own affinity group. They feel more comfortable together and they do, in fact, talk about some issues of race when they are together.

DOI: 10.4324/9781003508489-13

Ms. Cho feels conflicted about this request. On the one hand, she wants to support the girls in connecting, engaging, and building a community. Yet, she believes that gathering in the larger mixed-age group can also achieve these goals. Ms. Cho also feels a bit uncomfortable as the girls have requested that she participate in the lunch sessions; however, as an Asian American woman, Ms. Cho does not feel that this upholds the definition of affinity space if she does not share the same racial identity as the students.

Identity-Conscious Reflection Questions (to be done on your own and/or in group)

- What issues of identity do you notice in this scenario? What is it about your own identities and experiences that made you notice these issues?
- What identities in this scenario do you feel connected to? What identities in this scenario do you feel disconnected or distanced from?

Identity-Conscious Framework (to be discussed as a group)

- Name it: What are the problems or challenges in this scenario that are impacted by identity?
- Own it: Where do these problems or challenges come from? What are the possible reasons that these issues related to identity are emerging?
- Interrupt it: Centering the experiences of identity, what could occur to address barriers, worries, fears, or hesitations in this scenario? What steps could be taken to remedy the issues?
- Take responsibility: What is the follow up to this situation? What might have occurred differently if the people in the scenario were centering identity-consciousness?

Identity-Conscious Discussion Questions (to be discussed as a group)

- What did you notice about your group's process in talking about this case study? How might the identity of your group inform and impact your approach to this case study?

Additional Points to Consider (to be discussed as a group)

- The 8th graders in this scenario were the leaders of the Black Affinity Group. If the 7th graders separate into a different group and remove themselves from the larger affinity space, what impact might this have on leadership?

- What aspects of the larger institutional culture must be considered in this scenario? To what extent might this inform and impact other affinity groups? To what extent might that matter?
- As an Asian American, Ms. Cho noted that she feels she may be violating the affinity group norms if she participates with the 7th graders and does not share the same racial identity. What is the impact of this? What are possible equitable solutions that might address this issue?

Case 9.2: The National Guard

Briarwood High School is often the recipient of negative press due to its size, location, and demographics. As a predominantly Black and Brown public high school that has been significantly understaffed and under-resourced, there has been public and media attention to the increase in fighting between students during the school day. These fights have been recorded and shared on social media. While these issues have been going on for years, some shared on social media have raised the level of attention.

There is a consistent shortage of teachers and substitutes which leads students to be in study halls or unsupervised time in the hallways. Because teachers are often managing classes of thirty or more students, it is difficult to provide differentiated instruction in the classes to keep students engaged. Students have long complained about the crowded hallways, the lack of space and time to get fresh air during the day (e.g., recess), and the unsanitary conditions of bathrooms to name a few. There is a significant police presence already in the school, metal detectors at every entrance, and the hall monitors during passing times to move foot traffic along. Many parents and teachers have expressed concern that there are not enough adults in the building to address negative behaviors.

Some local activists who identify as people of color, frustrated at the lack of coordinated efforts to address these recurring incidents, requested that the state leaders send in the National Guard to help. With that announcement came heated conversations about this suggestion – some mention that bringing in this group to a predominantly Black/Brown high school is not the right move; others applaud the proposal as a potential solution to the shortage of adult supervision in the building. Local officials do not support the national guard coming into the school and who, up until this public attention, had not been very public or transparent about the needs of the school. Because of the attention, the news escalated to the governor of the state who announced a grant for the Briarwood School District to do a safety audit, and data is going to be collected about safety, supervision, and over-crowding to inform action moving forward.

Identity-Conscious Reflection Questions (to be done on your own and/or in group)

- What issues of identity do you notice in this scenario? What is it about your own identities and experiences that made you notice these issues?
- What identities in this scenario do you feel connected to? What identities in this scenario do you feel disconnected or distanced from?

Identity-Conscious Framework (to be discussed as a group)

- Name it: What are the problems or challenges in this scenario that are impacted by identity?
- Own it: Where do these problems or challenges come from? What are the possible reasons that these issues related to identity are emerging?
- Interrupt it: Centering the experiences of identity, what could occur to address barriers, worries, fears, or hesitations in this scenario? What steps could be taken to remedy the issues?
- Take responsibility: What is the follow up to this situation? What might have occurred differently if the people in the scenario were centering identity-consciousness?

Identity-Conscious Discussion Questions (to be discussed as a group)

- What did you notice about your group's process in talking about this case study? How might the identity of your group inform and impact your approach to this case study?

Additional Points to Consider

- The members of the city who brought forth the proposal to bring in the National Guard identify as people of color. What do you believe is the impact of their racial identities and this proposal?
- What factors may be contributing to the increased attention to Briarwood High School despite years of bringing these issues of safety, teacher shortages, and crowded classrooms?
- What is the impact of the safety measures (as stated in the case study) on the experiences of students at the school?

Case 9.3: A Place for Affinity

Rockaday Elementary School has taken steps to integrate issues of identity into their curriculum and celebrations at school. Before beginning any implementation, teachers and school leaders dedicated a year of professional development on understanding issues of identity – particularly issues of race – and writing curriculum in age appropriate levels. As the academic year was coming to a close, the school administrators and a few teachers met with the Parent Council to present some of the new initiatives for the next academic year. The team understood that parent and caregiver collaboration was key to a successful implementation.

As the administrative team and teachers presented to the parent council, many parents expressed concern with adding issues of identity into the curriculum, but trusted that the teachers and team leaders were thoughtful about the work. The administrative team and teachers included pathways for asking questions, for feedback, and for frequent check-ins with parents and caregivers that were pre-scheduled throughout the upcoming academic year.

As the meeting was coming to a close, a parent raised their hand to express concern that the teachers were advancing their knowledge of identity work, the students were going to receive lessons and engage in dialogues about this work, but that parents and caregivers lacked a comprehensive scope and sequence for themselves. A parent asked, "To what extent will there be workshops or opportunities for parents and caregivers to engage in this work? More specifically, as a white parent, what resources will the school be providing for me to learn about issues of identity and race so that I can support the learning that is happening at home? I know that some schools host affinity groups – where parents of the same identity come together to talk – will we have the opportunity to do this?"

Another parent quickly responded, "Oh, I hope we do not do affinity groups. The separation and segregation is part of the problem. If we are going to learn, we all need to learn together. I don't think having a group for white people and a group of people of color separately advances the work. If we move in the direction of having parent affinity groups, I certainly do not support this and cannot support a parent initiative that does this type of work."

Mrs. Davidson, a parent of a 3rd grader who identifies as Black, spoke up and said, "Do you understand that the entire day is actually an affinity group? My child is the only Black child in their 3rd grade classroom. Every single day *is* a white affinity group in their classroom. As a parent, whenever I come to third grade classroom events, I'm the only Black person in the entire room. It can feel very isolating, and I am an adult. So, yes, I need an affinity group. I need to see and talk to other Black parents here at this school. I firmly support any initiatives for affinity groups in our parent community."

At the end of the meeting, the administrative team and teachers gathered to debrief the situation. "I didn't even realize we were entertaining programming for parents," said one teacher. "Our focus was on children. What is going on with these parents? We aren't their therapists. We are their children's teachers." An administrator responded, "Well, I think there were some good points made here. While this was a small sample of parents, they do serve as leaders in the community. Maybe we should think about hosting affinity groups for parents. Maybe we host racial affinity groups for them." "But where does it stop?" asked another administrator. "If we offer affinity groups for race, what else are we opening the door to? And, do we actually have the capacity to do this type of work?"

Identity-Conscious Reflection Questions (to be done on your own and/or in group)

- What issues of identity do you notice in this scenario? What is it about your own identities and experiences that made you notice these issues?
- What identities in this scenario do you feel connected to? What identities in this scenario do you feel disconnected or distanced from?

Identity-Conscious Framework (to be discussed as a group)

- Name it: What are the problems or challenges in this scenario that are impacted by identity?
- Own it: Where do these problems or challenges come from? What are the possible reasons that these issues related to identity are emerging?
- Interrupt it: Centering the experiences of identity, what could occur to address barriers, worries, fears, or hesitations in this scenario? What steps could be taken to remedy the issues?
- Take responsibility: What is the follow up to this situation? What might have occurred differently if the people in the scenario were centering identity-consciousness?

Identity-Conscious Discussion Questions (to be discussed as a group)

- What did you notice about your group's process in talking about this case study? How might the identity of your group inform and impact your approach to this case study?

Additional Points to Consider

- One of the teachers made the comment, "We are not (the parents') therapists." Where is the boundary between home/school collaborative education programs and the social-emotional of parents and caregivers? What determines appropriate boundaries here? What protocols for decision-making occur in this area?
- How true or relevant is it that offering affinity groups for race might lead to the need or request for affinity groups of other identities and experiences? What is the impact of this?
- Providing programming for parents and caregivers often requires human and financial resources. To what extent does this factor into this type of decision-making?

Case 9.4: The Research Project

Mr. James has been teaching at the school for over fifteen years. One of the assignments that the students and the families look forward to is the independent research project that occurs in May. Students select an influential person who they learned about during the school year, research their lives and their contributions to society, and present a 5–7-minute oral presentation. The project is so beloved that Mr. James hosts a public event where families and former students can attend the presentations. In the past, audience members whisper with excitement, "Oh! That was the person I selected!" There is a great deal of joy and connection at the event.

Over the past year, as a part of the school professional development, Mr. James used the opportunity to examine the presentation project. He realized that all of the influential people selected shared one thing in common – every single one of the influential people the students selected were white. Mr. James realized that the students also chose individuals who he talked about in class. While they are all people of influence, Mr. James began to ask himself, "In addition to the current list of influential people who the students have selected, have my students learned about any influential people who are people of color?" Mr. James began to question what his role was in perpetuating this omission.

Knowing that the end of year project was informed by who he covered during the school year, Mr. James revised many of the lessons from September to April to include people of color. Now on the list, Mr. James has included the people of color that he covered on the list. When the time came to select individuals to present, Mr. James was disappointed to see that the students still only selected presentation subjects who are white. When he asked the students to share why they chose particular individuals, many of the students responded with, "My sibling did this presentation when they were in your class" or "My parents wanted me to choose this one."

The second year, Mr. James decided to take a more direct approach. He decided to only put of revisions, influential people of color on the list, which meant that students could only select people of color for their presentations. During the year, he continued to include people of color in his lessons and encouraged students to think about the May presentations. When the students saw the list, they were excited and began telling others who they had chosen.

The next day, Mr. James was called into the Principal's office. The Principal said she had received multiple emails and voicemails from parents and caregivers about the new list. Some expressed that they were disappointed their child could not continue the tradition of selecting the same influential person as their older sibling; others, more pointedly, remarked that only including people of color on the list was a form of "reverse racism." Mr. James is being asked to reconsider his assignment.

Identity-Conscious Reflection Questions (to be done on your own and/or in group)

- What issues of identity do you notice in this scenario? What is it about your own identities and experiences that made you notice these issues?
- What identities in this scenario do you feel connected to? What identities in this scenario do you feel disconnected or distanced from?

Identity-Conscious Framework (to be discussed as a group)

- Name it: What are the problems or challenges in this scenario that are impacted by identity?
- Own it: Where do these problems or challenges come from? What are the possible reasons that these issues related to identity are emerging?
- Interrupt it: Centering the experiences of identity, what could occur to address barriers, worries, fears, or hesitations in this scenario? What steps could be taken to remedy the issues?
- Take responsibility: What is the follow up to this situation? What might have occurred differently if the people in the scenario were centering identity-consciousness?

Identity-Conscious Discussion Questions (to be discussed as a group)

- What did you notice about your group's process in talking about this case study? How might the identity of your group inform and impact your approach to this case study?

Additional Points to Consider

- Mr. James examined his curriculum and assignment as a result of a school-wide initiative. To what extent should the school be supporting his decision?
- Traditions often connect a community. What is the role of traditions in this scenario? How might connections to traditions serve as an opportunity in this scenario?
- How might Mr. James or school leadership respond to the concerns that this new assignment perpetuates "reverse racism?"
- What is the role of agency for students in this scenario? What aspects of this scenario should students have been engaged or involved, if at all?

Case 9.5: A Parent and Administrator Clash

As a result of racial protest emerging from the 2020 reckoning in many schools, Excellence High School hired a Director of Diversity and Inclusion. The inaugural director, a Black woman named Sharra, was hired to address the experiences related to racism in the school. For three years, Sharra built relationships across the school community and was successful in creating buy-in for why issues of race – particularly the experiences of Black students – deserved the attention of the community. The work was ongoing, but Sharra made sure to pay attention to the multiple points of intersectionality that people experienced in the community. While the issues of race were central, Sharra also provided programming and support to many different clubs, organizations, and affinity groups on campus. Many important cross-identity coalitions were being built in the student community, and the students were beginning to see how their different identity groups often shared similar experiences.

Following the conflicts and increasing violence in the region of Israel, Palestine, Gaza, and neighboring countries, a growing vocal community of parents demanded that Sharra address anti-semitism at the school. As the violence progressed week after week, a dozen parents requested a meeting with the Principal and Sharra and demanded that the school community hear from the Administration that the school "denounce terrorist actions and express unwavering support for Israel." When the Principal and Sharra stated that the school had an existing policy against commenting on issues that were rooted in international issues, the parents responded that "the Administration did not understand what it means to be historically marginalized, have violence perpetrated on their people, and have no one stand up for them."

Later that afternoon, Sharra met with the Principal to debrief the meeting. In that meeting, Sharra expressed concern that, as a Black woman, she had to sit in that meeting and be accused of "not understanding what it meant to be marginalized, to have violence perpetrated on their people, and have no one stand up for them." While the Principal agreed with Sharra in this private meeting, Sharra was disappointed that the Principal did not say anything to the parents during the meeting about the inappropriateness of the comment.

Identity-Conscious Reflection Questions (to be done on your own and/or in group)

- What issues of identity do you notice in this scenario? What is it about your own identities and experiences that made you notice these issues?
- What identities in this scenario do you feel connected to? What identities in this scenario do you feel disconnected or distanced from?

Identity-Conscious Framework (to be discussed as a group)

- Name it: What are the problems or challenges in this scenario that are impacted by identity?
- Own it: Where do these problems or challenges come from? What are the possible reasons that these issues related to identity are emerging?
- Interrupt it: Centering the experiences of identity, what could occur to address barriers, worries, fears, or hesitations in this scenario? What steps could be taken to remedy the issues?
- Take responsibility: What is the follow up to this situation? What might have occurred differently if the people in the scenario were centering identity-consciousness?

Identity-Conscious Discussion Questions (to be discussed as a group)

- What did you notice about your group's process in talking about this case study? How might the identity of your group inform and impact your approach to this case study?

Additional Points to Consider

- The identity of the Principal was not mentioned in the case study. How might this inform and impact the scenario? What informs your belief about this?
- What might the Principal have said during the meeting to address the comments of the parents? What would have been the impact on Sharra? On the parents?
- How might the school policy on "not commenting on international issues" be helpful? How might it be limiting?
- What do you believe follows this scenario? How might identity inform and impact a strategy that addresses what comes next?
- How might the rise of anti-semitism as well as Islamophobia inform the school's response?

10

Case Studies on Socioeconomic Status

Chapter at a Glance

This chapter presents five case studies related to class and socioeconomic status. Readers are encouraged to review the case study, engage in reflective practice using the guided questions provided, and participate in peer learning communities for dialogue. The goal is not to solve the case but rather practice slowing down, using an identity-conscious lens, and creating action for future use.

Case 10.1: The Birthday Party

At Knowles Elementary School, there has been a commitment to providing greater equity in the community. One area that the administration and teachers identified as an ongoing issue of inequity is related to birthday parties. In the past, a child's family hosted a birthday party and invited a select group of students over to their house or out to a special event (e.g., pizza party, movie afternoon). Some families, mostly of children who were not invited to these parties, felt these practices were setting up situations of exclusion as children handed out invitations during the school day and recounted how fun the party was at recess or lunch times.

In an effort to provide greater inclusion and equity, the administrative team and teachers strongly encouraged families to host birthday parties only if everyone in the class is invited. From that point on, students were encouraged to bring in birthday invitations for every child in the class.

While this appeared to have been a good solution, a number of families complained that this recommendation actually prohibited their families from hosting a birthday celebration. Some families mentioned that they did not have the financial means to invite everyone from the class nor did they live in houses or apartments that could host that many children. In addition, renting an external venue was not an option due to financial obligations. And, for children who had birthdays in the winter months, hosting a birthday party in an open setting like a playground or park was unrealistic.

The administrative team and teachers regrouped and decided that they needed to send a strong message about how children felt about being excluded from these traditions. They decided that each month, they would have class families bring in treats to celebrate the children who have birthdays during that month (in June, they would celebrate summer time birthdays). Families also pushed back on this practice as some parents and caregivers brought in homemade cupcakes while others brought in elaborate goody bags and treats.

The administrative team and teachers wondered if it was possible at all to address the issue of birthdays and celebrations.

Identity-Conscious Reflection Questions (to be done on your own and/or in group)

- What issues of identity do you notice in this scenario? What is it about your own identities and experiences that made you notice these issues?
- What identities in this scenario do you feel connected to? What identities in this scenario do you feel disconnected or distanced from?

Identity-Conscious Framework (to be discussed as a group)

- Name it: What are the problems or challenges in this scenario that are impacted by identity?
- Own it: Where do these problems or challenges come from? What are the possible reasons that these issues related to identity are emerging?
- Interrupt it: Centering the experiences of identity, what could occur to address barriers, worries, fears, or hesitations in this scenario? What steps could be taken to remedy the issues?

> ◆ Take responsibility: What is the follow up to this situation? What might have occurred differently if the people in the scenario were centering identity-consciousness?
>
> **Identity-Conscious Discussion Questions (to be discussed as a group)**
> ◆ What did you notice about your group's process in talking about this case study? How might the identity of your group inform and impact your approach to this case study?

Case 10.2: The Payscale

Trina is in her sixth year as a teacher at Carter Middle School. She teaches 5th grade, is an advisor, a club leader for the Latinx Student Affinity Group, and volunteers in the after-school theater program. Trina's family is a few states away, but she travels home often. She has been transparent that her salary supports not only herself but also her mom, dad, and brother living in her hometown. When she returns home each month, Trina gives her family money for their bills, rent, and other expenses. Trina knows that teachers at school get together for drinks and dinners. Even though she is invited, Trina always declines because she is on a very tight budget. She knows that the children she teaches come from wealthy families and send them to private schools like Carter Middle School where the yearly tuition is more than her annual salary.

Trina has never complained about her salary as a teacher. After all, what she makes each year is more than anyone else in her family has ever made. She is the first in her family to graduate from college and earn her master's degree, and she has always believed the salary she was making was more than fair. When she was offered the job and told the salary, she accepted the offer and did not negotiate.

At Carter Middle School, there has been a commitment to diversify the teaching community. To do so, the principal has formed a few different hiring committees to focus on both hiring qualified teachers and increasing racial diversity. One step in the process was to ask committees to evaluate the current job postings and make sure they are attractive to a diverse population of candidates. Trina was thrilled to be asked. She sat down at her desk, opened her computer, and pulled up the job posting. She had some suggestions about the text of the job postings that included the mission and vision of the school as well as a few changes to the requirements. When Trina got to the end of the posting and saw the salary, she was confused. The posted salary for an entry-level teacher was $6,000 more than she was currently making, even with five years of experience at the school. Trina wants to say something to her principal, but her parents have advised her to just be grateful she is making a good salary. They fear that speaking up might make her boss upset and it would be a risk to lose her job.

Identity-Conscious Reflection Questions (to be done on your own and/or in group)

- What issues of identity do you notice in this scenario? What is it about your own identities and experiences that made you notice these issues?
- What identities in this scenario do you feel connected to? What identities in this scenario do you feel disconnected or distanced from?

Identity-Conscious Framework (to be discussed as a group)

- Name it: What are the problems or challenges in this scenario that are impacted by identity?
- Own it: Where do these problems or challenges come from? What are the possible reasons that these issues related to identity are emerging?
- Interrupt it: Centering the experiences of identity, what could occur to address barriers, worries, fears, or hesitations in this scenario? What steps could be taken to remedy the issues?
- Take responsibility: What is the follow up to this situation? What might have occurred differently if the people in the scenario were centering identity-consciousness?

Identity-Conscious Discussion Questions (to be discussed as a group)

- What did you notice about your group's process in talking about this case study? How might the identity of your group inform and impact your approach to this case study?

Additional Points to Consider

- What might the principal have considered before asking people to do work on the hiring committee?
- What might Trina do or say to address this situation?
- The National Labor Relations Act makes it illegal in the US to prohibit employees from discussing wages, in most cases. What do you think Trina would experience if she asked other teachers in her experience range what their salaries were?
- What is the role of Trina's family in this case?

Case 10.3: Difference Within

Julie was excited to finally be in college and meeting new people. She had attended the same small private school for her entire K-12 education and needed to see some new faces, learn new stories, and have new conversations. At the activities fair, Julie immediately saw the Black Student Union table and approached the student leaders to learn more. The students at the table were warm and welcoming and told her to come to the first meeting.

The evening of the meeting, Julie was arrived late. She had been in classes all day, was exhausted, and had not eaten since early morning. When she got to the meeting, she was overwhelmed with how many people were already there. There didn't seem to be others who were lost – like she felt – but that everyone had found their groups. A student across the room waved her over to join them.

When she got to the group, she introduced herself. Everyone seemed nice and did the same. One student said, "Okay, now let me give you the road map of this room. Over there – those are the East Coast kids who all went to private boarding schools. Over there are the Black international students who do not like being lumped into things with Black Americans. That group there – those are the students from the Caribbean. Oh, and that group right there, that group is special. Don't bother with them. Those are the 'Jack and Jill' students. They are the children of *Who's Who* in wealthy Black society. They'll talk your ear off about their galas and fundraising and leadership – always acting better than the rest of us just because they come from rich families. They always come up in these meetings like they own the place." The rest of the group laughed and nodded in agreement.

Julie grew uncomfortable but kept a smile on her face. She grew up going to Jack and Jill events which her family saw as an important leadership opportunity. She made great friends through that group, and she was able to spend meaningful time with her parents as a result of their activities. She certainly did not think she was better than anyone, but wondered if this is how others saw the organization that played a pivotal role in her teenage years. She is not sure if she should say anything to this group of new friends.

> **Identity-Conscious Reflection Questions (to be done on your own and/or in group)**
> ♦ What issues of identity do you notice in this scenario? What is it about your own identities and experiences that made you notice these issues?

- What identities in this scenario do you feel connected to? What identities in this scenario do you feel disconnected or distanced from?

Identity-Conscious Framework (to be discussed as a group)

- Name it: What are the problems or challenges in this scenario that are impacted by identity?
- Own it: Where do these problems or challenges come from? What are the possible reasons that these issues related to identity are emerging?
- Interrupt it: Centering the experiences of identity, what could occur to address barriers, worries, fears, or hesitations in this scenario? What steps could be taken to remedy the issues?
- Take responsibility: What is the follow up to this situation? What might have occurred differently if the people in the scenario were centering identity-consciousness?

Identity-Conscious Discussion Questions (to be discussed as a group)

- What did you notice about your group's process in talking about this case study? How might the identity of your group inform and impact your approach to this case study?

Additional Points to Consider

- What might contribute to Julie not speaking up in this group?
- What assumptions are others making about socioeconomic status in this scenario?
- What do you think would happen if she moved over to be with some of her peers from the Jack and Jill group?
- What do you believe are the challenges and opportunities in working with such a diverse group of people even in an affinity/identity space?

Case 10.4: The Soup Kitchen

Each year, East Country Day School hosts a day of service for the students, faculty, and families. The community service committee chooses a dozen different organizations to partner with and sets up transportation. You are one of the chaperones on this service day, and you have been assigned to take 20 students and families to the Hope House, a service organization in the heart of the city focused on providing fresh food to those in need. During the lunch shift, participants can expect to serve over sixty people who may be experiencing food insecurity.

When you and the volunteers arrived, the Director of Hope House gave a brief orientation. He told the volunteers about the mission of Hope House – to serve those in need with dignity, compassion, and respect. Volunteers were prepped about food service, cleanliness, and cross-contamination. But more importantly, the Director explained that "We can't always know what people are going through, so we must treat everyone kindly as a guest of Hope House. They might experience judgment outside of these walls, but here in Hope House, we deliver radical hospitality."

The students and families lined up at their stations and were given their responsibilities for the lunch shift. As guests of Hope House arrived, the students were friendly, warm, and engaging. As the chaperone, you were so proud of the behavior of the students. During the shift, a few students approached you and expressed how being in community at Hope House was an important learning experience. Even after the shift ended and the final guest left, the students continued to buzz with excitement. After helping to clean up, you, the students, and the families boarded the bus back to East Country Day.

On the bus, you asked everyone about their experiences and what they noticed and felt while they were serving. Many responded that being at Hope House gave them new insight into food insecurity, that it felt good to serve, and that places like Hope were important. Just as you were pulling into the school parking lot, one parent spoke up and said, "I definitely enjoyed it. But I did get annoyed that some people didn't belong there. I saw some people coming through the line with Apple watches. I even saw one woman with a Coach bag. There was even a man wearing a suit there! I can't believe the nerve of some people just looking for a free lunch instead of making room for those who really need it. Hope House should really only let in people who need the help." She said this loud enough for everyone to hear, and looked around the bus for signs of affirmation.

At that moment, the bus doors opened and everyone filed out.

Identity-Conscious Reflection Questions (to be done on your own and/or in group)

- ◆ What issues of identity do you notice in this scenario? What is it about your own identities and experiences that made you notice these issues?
- ◆ What identities in this scenario do you feel connected to? What identities in this scenario do you feel disconnected or distanced from?

Identity-Conscious Framework (to be discussed as a group)

- Name it: What are the problems or challenges in this scenario that are impacted by identity?
- Own it: Where do these problems or challenges come from? What are the possible reasons that these issues related to identity are emerging?
- Interrupt it: Centering the experiences of identity, what could occur to address barriers, worries, fears, or hesitations in this scenario? What steps could be taken to remedy the issues?
- Take responsibility: What is the follow up to this situation? What might have occurred differently if the people in the scenario were centering identity-consciousness?

Identity-Conscious Discussion Questions (to be discussed as a group)

- What did you notice about your group's process in talking about this case study? How might the identity of your group inform and impact your approach to this case study?

Additional Points to Consider

- What follow up, if any, with the parent is necessary?
- What do you believe the other participants may have taken away from that statement?
- How might stereotypes about class inform and impact the parent's comments?
- What, if at all, is the follow up from the school? Does it change that the commenter was a parent rather than a student?

Case 10.5: Art Supplies

Jay's high school offers International Baccalaureate (IB) classes. The program is different from the existing high school curriculum due to its heavy emphasis on projects, processes, and inquiry. Students are often working on a set of projects over the course of two years and are tasked with a series of independent work.

Jay's IB art class is focused on self-directed projects. Jay decided to use yarn and crochet as a medium for their final project. When Jay asked the art teacher if the school had any supplies, the art teacher responded with, "We don't have anything that you'd need. However, if you want to shift to something like charcoal art or painting, we have some things in the closet for you to use." Jay went to the closet and saw paintbrushes that were missing hairs, charcoal bits and pieces, and erasers that were hard as a rock. Jay affirmed with the teacher that these were the supplies that the class was supposed to use for their IB art projects, and Jay's teacher said, "Yes, unless you want to buy your own."

Jay went home that day and asked his parents if he could purchase some supplies. Jay's parents, who can easily afford materials without pulling from another budget, brought Jay to the craft store and told him to pick out whatever he needed. Jay purchased new crochet hooks and over $100 worth of yarn.

Jay worked independently for a few weeks. In the third week, the students were asked to bring their projects-in-progress so the teacher could review what they were doing. Many of Jay's classmates were impressed by Jay's work, the amount of material Jay had, and how elaborate the design was. When others presented their projects, they each shared how hard it was to get the projects done because they did not have access to materials. Many of the students used the supplies from the art room closet. Jay knew those were inadequate and chose not to use them.

Jay left class that day realizing that, while he worked hard on his project, he certainly had opportunities others did not. Jay approached the art teacher after class and said, "I don't think this is quite fair. I mean, I worked hard, but how difficult was it really for me to just go and buy things? Knowing this is a project to pass a major course of study, this just seems entirely unfair."

Identity-Conscious Reflection Questions (to be done on your own and/or in group)

- What issues of identity do you notice in this scenario? What is it about your own identities and experiences that made you notice these issues?
- What identities in this scenario do you feel connected to? What identities in this scenario do you feel disconnected or distanced from?

Identity-Conscious Framework (to be discussed as a group)

- Name it: What are the problems or challenges in this scenario that are impacted by identity?

- Own it: Where do these problems or challenges come from? What are the possible reasons that these issues related to identity are emerging?
- Interrupt it: Centering the experiences of identity, what could occur to address barriers, worries, fears, or hesitations in this scenario? What steps could be taken to remedy the issues?
- Take responsibility: What is the follow up to this situation? What might have occurred differently if the people in the scenario were centering identity-consciousness?

Identity-Conscious Discussion Questions (to be discussed as a group)
- What did you notice about your group's process in talking about this case study? How might the identity of your group inform and impact your approach to this case study?

Additional Points to Consider
- How does inequity show up in the art class?
- Are there opportunities the art teacher can take given the limited resources?
- How might grading issues be impacted by access to supplies, particularly when the final project relies so heavily on supplies?
- What might the students do to address the existing inequities?
- What occurs if there is no funding for these supplies for students? What options exist as a result of this?

11

Case Studies on Religion/Faith

Chapter at a Glance

This chapter presents five case studies related to religion/faith. Readers are encouraged to review the case study, engage in reflective practice using the guided questions provided, and participate in peer learning communities for dialogue. The goal is not to solve the case but rather practice slowing down, using an identity-conscious lens, and creating action for future use.

Case 11.1: Song Choice and Choir

Michelle is a student who enjoys singing and who hopes to major in vocal performance in college. In order to create a competitive college portfolio, Michelle has signed up for every opportunity that her school has to offer: choir, acapella group, voice lessons, and talent shows. Of all the different avenues for performance, Michelle most loves choir. She finds singing in a group, practicing together, and filling a room with harmonies and melodies to be moving.

Michelle's family is also very religious. While the music choices in elementary and middle school never posed an issue, Michelle's parents have realized that some of the songs they sing in choir and in the high school acapella group do not align with their religious beliefs. They see the benefit of singing in a group, practicing together, and building friendships; however, some of the choices in the upper school seem to include more references to pop culture, relationships, and identity that her parents are not as comfortable with.

Michelle's parents asked to speak with the choir director about the choice of music the choir sings. They want to encourage the choir director to choose different songs so as not to put Michelle in the position of having to choose to stay in choir or to quit. The choir director believes that Michelle's parents are making too much of the meaning of the songs and is offended that anyone would believe they would choose songs that are inappropriate or send a negative message about identity and/or relationships. The choir director suggested that Michelle not continue with choir given that she already has other opportunities to sing.

Michelle's parents elevated this conversation to the principal and the dean of faculty. They believe that the choir director's response was insensitive and inappropriate and disadvantages Michelle from the opportunity to build her skill and to be competitive in a college portfolio.

Identity-Conscious Reflection Questions (to be done on your own and/or in group)

- What issues of identity do you notice in this scenario? What is it about your own identities and experiences that made you notice these issues?
- What identities in this scenario do you feel connected to? What identities in this scenario do you feel disconnected or distanced from?

Identity-Conscious Framework (to be discussed as a group)

- Name it: What are the problems or challenges in this scenario that are impacted by identity?
- Own it: Where do these problems or challenges come from? What are the possible reasons that these issues related to identity are emerging?
- Interrupt it: Centering the experiences of identity, what could occur to address barriers, worries, fears, or hesitations in this scenario? What steps could be taken to remedy the issues?
- Take responsibility: What is the follow up to this situation? What might have occurred differently if the people in the scenario were centering identity-consciousness?

> **Identity-Conscious Discussion Questions (to be discussed as a group)**
> - What did you notice about your group's process in talking about this case study? How might the identity of your group inform and impact your approach to this case study?
>
> **Additional Points to Consider**
> - To what extent should the choir director have considered the identities of the students in the choir when selecting songs?
> - Is there a need to be transparent about the differences between the music selections in lower/middle school and the upper school students?
> - What assumptions are each of the constituents making about each other in this scenario?
> - How does the topic of religion and religious practices tend to play out in your school?

Case 11.2: The Dining Hall

In an effort to be more inclusive in their food options, Dining Services at West College began hosting specific times and locations that served halal and kosher meals. In the first few days of the new menus, there was significant interest in dining in these locations. Many students were curious about the food and about a new offering at West. Over the next few weeks, however, attendance and dining decreased. At each meal, between 15–25 students came to the dining halls despite the staff preparing meals for up to 100+ people each time block. Dining Services knew that change takes time and that eventually they would see a pattern and scale accordingly.

Each week, however, the dining services staff noticed that they were preparing meals for fewer students. One day, only five students came to the dining hall location. After assessing the data of the halal and kosher meals initiative, the school and dining services agreed that they would no longer be able to offer this specific service. Upon the announcement of a return to a full dining menu, the attendance filled back up to capacity and stayed there the rest of the week.

Upon the announcement of the change of the dining hall to return to a full menu for dining, some students expressed frustration that the halal and kosher hall was the only place they could eat in alignment with their practices. They drew on the school's stated commitment to equity, saying that "removing opportunities for students to eat in a kosher and halal space was inequitable as members of this student body." They asked others to join them in protest and to persuade Dining Services to bring back a kosher and halal dining space. They noted that first year students were required to live on campus and purchase full dining plans, yet some had to order food from off campus in order to meet their dietary and religious practices.

The administration agreed that the efforts to provide halal and kosher dining was to advance greater equity; yet, it was not sustainable.

Identity-Conscious Reflection Questions (to be done on your own and/or in group)
- What issues of identity do you notice in this scenario? What is it about your own identities and experiences that made you notice these issues?
- What identities in this scenario do you feel connected to? What identities in this scenario do you feel disconnected or distanced from?

Identity-Conscious Framework (to be discussed as a group)
- Name it: What are the problems or challenges in this scenario that are impacted by identity?
- Own it: Where do these problems or challenges come from? What are the possible reasons that these issues related to identity are emerging?
- Interrupt it: Centering the experiences of identity, what could occur to address barriers, worries, fears, or hesitations in this scenario? What steps could be taken to remedy the issues?
- Take responsibility: What is the follow up to this situation? What might have occurred differently if the people in the scenario were centering identity-consciousness?

Identity-Conscious Discussion Questions (to be discussed as a group)
- What did you notice about your group's process in talking about this case study? How might the identity of your group inform and impact your approach to this case study?

Additional Points to Consider
- What other dining options might be possible on a campus to provide for students who observe specific dietary and food practices?
- How often do financial implications guide decisions? To what extent might there be exceptions?
- What is the role of student voice in presenting initiatives? What might have been addressed if students were at the center of the decision making?

Case 11.3: Read Aloud

After the COVID-19 pandemic, Ms. Henry noticed that the students seemed less and less engaged around reading for pleasure. She decided that, in addition to her existing curriculum, Ms. Henry would choose a book that was based on or closely resembled a movie that the students likely have seen. This year, she chose to read a fantasy book that featured characters of color as the main leads. The book centers around a mystical school where the characters perform magic spells, practice rituals they read in books, and summon different creatures from beyond. The students look forward to the read-aloud time and are often overheard talking about the book during lunch and recess.

Mr. and Mrs. Rhodes have a child in Ms. Henry's class. They asked to set up a meeting with her about the book choice. The Rhodes family was very supportive of the fact that Ms. Henry chose a book that centered characters of color as diversity is an issue they are deeply committed to. They also have noticed their own child's joy of reading escalate as he talks about the book at dinner and tells his family about the story. Mr. and Mrs. Rhodes, however, are concerned about the content. As a religious family, they do not want their child reading stories about magic, mysticism, and creatures from the beyond. In their belief, doing so brings about evil and ill.

They do not want to discourage Ms. Henry from doing what seems to be meeting the needs of many of the students. At the same time, they certainly do not want their own child to be exposed to the text nor to be left out of the experience. They do not want their child to be given an alternative task, to leave the room, nor to sit and listen to the story. They have expressed that honoring and respecting diversity must also include their religious practices, beliefs, and requests.

Identity-Conscious Reflection Questions (to be done on your own and/or in group)

- What issues of identity do you notice in this scenario? What is it about your own identities and experiences that made you notice these issues?
- What identities in this scenario do you feel connected to? What identities in this scenario do you feel disconnected or distanced from?

Identity-Conscious Framework (to be discussed as a group)

- Name it: What are the problems or challenges in this scenario that are impacted by identity?

- Own it: Where do these problems or challenges come from? What are the possible reasons that these issues related to identity are emerging?
- Interrupt it: Centering the experiences of identity, what could occur to address barriers, worries, fears, or hesitations in this scenario? What steps could be taken to remedy the issues?
- Take responsibility: What is the follow up to this situation? What might have occurred differently if the people in the scenario were centering identity-consciousness?

Identity-Conscious Discussion Questions (to be discussed as a group)

- What did you notice about your group's process in talking about this case study? How might the identity of your group inform and impact your approach to this case study?

Additional Points to Consider

- Different faith traditions may view content related to fantasy, witchcraft, and magic as not aligned with their beliefs.
- The approach Ms. Henry is taking in the classroom seems to be working in terms of the student excitement about reading. What, if at all, do you believe is being asked of her?
- While the parents do not want their child to be removed from the activity, what other options can you identify that would keep the student engaged and still read the book?
- What aspects of identity should Ms. Henry consider for the next book?

Case 11.4: World Events

In recent weeks, a major international incident has broken out onto the world stage. While it is an event that primarily impacts a particular geographic region, the effects are felt here in the United States and in our communities. There are families and students who have relatives in that geographic region, and some of the conflict has to do with religion and faith.

It has not been the habit at the school to comment on international events. Your administrative team has sent out a community-wide email when incidents here in the United States have impacted the way people are experiencing the world, but they have not consistently commented on global events. There is currently no policy in the handbook about community-wide emails.

There has been pressure from different families for the school to send out a community-wide email message that denounces what is happening in another part of the world. The administrative team has stayed true to their practice of not sending out a communication. However, the pressure to do so is mounting. Many families disagree with the administrative team that what is occurring in a different region has no impact. In fact, because part of this event is rooted in religion and faith, a number of families believe that their own faith traditions are being questioned and challenged.

The administrative team, along with the communications team, decided to send an email acknowledging what was happening and affirming the school's mission of "honoring the humanity of all and working towards peaceful solutions." They believed that rooting the message in the school's mission and values was a helpful way to address the situation. Immediately after the email went out, families were calling and leaving angry messages that said the communication did not go far enough. They wanted the administrative team to send a clear message and to take a side in this global issue. And, that saying we "honored the humanity of all" was similar to saying "all lives matter" in response to the recent Black Lives Matter movement. The families alluded to threats ranging from pulling their children out of the school, withdrawing on promised pledges and funding, and going to the local news to shame the school's leaders for their response.

Identity-Conscious Reflection Questions (to be done on your own and/or in group):

- What issues of identity do you notice in this scenario? What is it about your own identities and experiences that made you notice these issues?
- What identities in this scenario do you feel connected to? What identities in this scenario do you feel disconnected or distanced from?

Identity-Conscious Framework (to be discussed as a group)

- Name it: What are the problems or challenges in this scenario that are impacted by identity?
- Own it: Where do these problems or challenges come from? What are the possible reasons that these issues related to identity are emerging?
- Interrupt it: Centering the experiences of identity, what could occur to address barriers, worries, fears, or hesitations in this scenario? What steps could be taken to remedy the issues?

- Take responsibility: What is the follow up to this situation? What might have occurred differently if the people in the scenario were centering identity-consciousness?

Identity-Conscious Discussion Questions (to be discussed as a group)
- What did you notice about your group's process in talking about this case study? How might the identity of your group inform and impact your approach to this case study?

Additional Points to Consider
- What do you believe is the role of school/education in addressing global issues?
- Do you believe there should be a policy in place for communicating about issues (e.g., which kind, how, where)?
- What do you believe is the purpose of the alluded threats such as funding, enrollment, and publicity?
- How might teachers and school leaders address the pressure from families to "take a side"?

Case 11.5: Freedom to Express

Brace High School has a diverse student community with affinity groups for students of color, LGBTQ students, students with disabilities, and international students. For the most part, the student body is politically active and there are typically activities that encourage acceptance and belonging of minoritized groups.

The LGBTQ+ Alliance wanted to hold a Day of (No) Silence – a nationally led student movement to protest discrimination and harassment of LGBTQ+ people. The group created marketing posters and planned an optional assembly for students to learn about the movement, meet other students who identify as LGBTQ+ and allies, and experience a sense of community focused on these issues.

On that same day, a few students arrived at school wearing t-shirts quoting select Bible verses that condemn homosexuality. They were met with mixed reactions from their peers – some reacting out of shock and others out of anger. The students were called in to the Administration Office and asked about their shirts. The students said that wearing the shirts is a freedom of their expression and they had a right to them. The administrator stated that their shirts constituted harassment and wearing them interrupted the learning environment at school. The students disagreed and stated that having an entire school day dedicated to LGBTQ+ political movement, including an assembly, went against their own religious beliefs and that created a hostile school day for them.

Identity-Conscious Reflection Questions (to be done on your own and/or in group)
- What issues of identity do you notice in this scenario? What is it about your own identities and experiences that made you notice these issues?
- What identities in this scenario do you feel connected to? What identities in this scenario do you feel disconnected or distanced from?

Identity-Conscious Framework (to be discussed as a group)
- Name it: What are the problems or challenges in this scenario that are impacted by identity?
- Own it: Where do these problems or challenges come from? What are the possible reasons that these issues related to identity are emerging?
- Interrupt it: Centering the experiences of identity, what could occur to address barriers, worries, fears, or hesitations in this scenario? What steps could be taken to remedy the issues?
- Take responsibility: What is the follow up to this situation? What might have occurred differently if the people in the scenario were centering identity-consciousness?

Identity-Conscious Discussion Questions (to be discussed as a group)
- What did you notice about your group's process in talking about this case study? How might the identity of your group inform and impact your approach to this case study?

Additional Points to Consider
- In 2006, a similar incident sparked the case *Harper v Poway Unified School District*. The findings stated that having the student remove the shirt was not a violation of First Amendment Rights. However, in a dissenting opinion, the judge stated that choosing to protect the Day of Silence meant that the school was choosing sides on a highly controversial issue and stifling religious expression.
- How might this have been handled at your school? What conditions create these types of behaviors?
- How might your school manage cases like this via the school handbook? Through advisory programs?

12

Case Studies on Disability

Chapter at a Glance

This chapter presents five case studies related to disability. Readers are encouraged to review the case study, engage in reflective practice using the guided questions provided, and participate in peer learning communities for dialogue. The goal is not to solve the case but rather practice slowing down, using an identity-conscious lens, and creating action for future use.

Case 12.1: Recommendations for Employment

Mr. Nicholson is the Upper Division Principal at a school. He is wrapping up his hiring process and offered the position to his top candidate, Ms. Angelo, for the Director of Student Culture, a student-facing position that supports the advisors and student programs. Ms. Angelo meets all of the requirements for the position and brings a great deal of experience and insight to the role.

After Ms. Angelo was offered the position, she signed the contract that affirmed she could complete all of the duties as assigned. Upon returning the contract, Ms. Angelo disclosed to Mr. Nicholson that she lives with a chronic illness that may impact her ability to physically come to work in person. She mentioned she is available to log in and hold meetings virtually on days she is unable to come in. Because her chronic illness involves unpredictable flare ups, she is unable to predict when she will be in person.

DOI: 10.4324/9781003508489-16

Ms. Angelo affirms that she is a dedicated worker who will always come in when she is able. However, it is important that she has the flexibility to work from home when it is not physically possible for her to come to work.

Mr. Nicholson asked for her permission to tell the other members of the Administrative Team about her possible need to work online at times. While most were understanding and wanted to be as supportive as possible, others brought up that this would be a deviation from what is considered the norm at the school. One administrator stated, "This type of position really does require that the person is available to students and to advisors when issues arise. How will this person be available if they are at home?" Mr. Nicholson assured the team members that, because of lessons we learned during COVID-19, we know that the technology is reliable for being able to connect with each other. Another administrator pushed back and said, "Yes, but we are no longer working with COVID-19 restrictions. We are back in person, and I just don't see how an administrator can support a community if they are out of the building."

Mr. Nicholson is confident he made the right decision hiring Ms. Angelo. He is struggling to figure out how to communicate about Ms. Angelo's schedule, to support her transition to the community, and to meet the needs of the school community who benefit from having a leader easily accessible in cases of emergency or need.

Identity-Conscious Reflection Questions (to be done on your own and/or in group)

- What issues of identity do you notice in this scenario? What is it about your own identities and experiences that made you notice these issues?
- What identities in this scenario do you feel connected to? What identities in this scenario do you feel disconnected or distanced from?

Identity-Conscious Framework (to be discussed as a group)

- Name it: What are the problems or challenges in this scenario that are impacted by identity?
- Own it: Where do these problems or challenges come from? What are the possible reasons that these issues related to identity are emerging?
- Interrupt it: Centering the experiences of identity, what could occur to address barriers, worries, fears, or hesitations in this scenario? What steps could be taken to remedy the issues?

- Take responsibility: What is the follow up to this situation? What might have occurred differently if the people in the scenario were centering identity-consciousness?

Identity-Conscious Discussion Questions (to be discussed as a group)
- What did you notice about your group's process in talking about this case study? How might the identity of your group inform and impact your approach to this case study?

Additional Points to Consider
- Job descriptions are detailed contracts that outline the requirements for particular positions. What might be missing from this job description that would inform or impact whether or not Ms. Angelo could meet the needs of the position?
- Knowing that processes during COVID-19 heavily relied on people not being in the same building, what thoughts or attitudes might people be presenting as they push back on Ms. Angelo's schedule accommodations?
- What key points should Mr. Nicholson consider in order to create a healthy transition for Ms. Angelo into the community? How might this best be communicated?
- What conflicts and risks might Mr. Nicolson need to address in order to shift negative attitudes about this situation?

Case 12.2: The Theater Performance

Jason has often remarked, "If it weren't for the theater program, I wouldn't even bother showing up for school." Jason's life is theater. After high school, Jason plans on going to a performing arts college and then try his shot at Broadway. "If I can make it there, I can make it anywhere", Jason frequently says.

Jason's school is known for doing very well in the statewide theater competitions, and Jason has been one of the major leads in each play since his 9th grade year. As a 12th grader, this performance not only will be his last at the high school level, but he was hoping to film some of the scenes to include in a portfolio.

When the theater director announced the play for the season, the students were not familiar with it. The director, Mr. Jones, handed out the scripts, assigned parts, and asked everyone to have it read by the end of the week. Jason never really cared about what show was chosen – he just couldn't wait to get on stage.

While reading the script at home, Jason realized that there were some pretty outdated words and sentiments in the play. Specifically, the play had a number of references to people with disabilities as being "retarded" and "stupid." Jason's character, in particular, was often the one saying these lines and disparaging other characters in the play by using offensive language.

Later that week at the read-through, Jason raised his hand at the beginning of the session and said he was really uncomfortable with the language used in the play and that he would be the one delivering the lines. The theater director assured him that, "That's just how they talked when this play took place" and "Everyone knows it's just acting – no one actually is going to believe you think those things." Jason continued on with rehearsal, growing increasingly uncomfortable as he said the lines aloud. After rehearsal, Jason spoke to a few other castmates and asked their opinion. "Mr. Jones never would have picked a play if it was that offensive. Just trust him." Another said, "Like he said, it's just acting. No one really believes these things."

The words of his castmates and director were not comforting. The next morning, Jason asked the director if it were possible for him to change some lines or maybe substitute the offensive words for abbreviations. The director said, "Absolutely not."

Jason had a lot on the line in terms of his future plans for college and his passion for theater. He needed to make a decision about what to do next.

Identity-Conscious Reflection Questions (to be done on your own and/or in group)

- What issues of identity do you notice in this scenario? What is it about your own identities and experiences that made you notice these issues?
- What identities in this scenario do you feel connected to? What identities in this scenario do you feel disconnected or distanced from?

Identity-Conscious Framework (to be discussed as a group)

- Name it: What are the problems or challenges in this scenario that are impacted by identity?
- Own it: Where do these problems or challenges come from? What are the possible reasons that these issues related to identity are emerging?

- Interrupt it: Centering the experiences of identity, what could occur to address barriers, worries, fears, or hesitations in this scenario? What steps could be taken to remedy the issues?
- Take responsibility: What is the follow up to this situation? What might have occurred differently if the people in the scenario were centering identity-consciousness?

Identity-Conscious Discussion Questions (to be discussed as a group)

- What did you notice about your group's process in talking about this case study? How might the identity of your group inform and impact your approach to this case study?

Additional Points to Consider

- What are the key decision points from Jason's perspective?
- What is the role of the theater director in this process?
- How might the theater director have responded differently? What might have been the impact of that response?
- Jason's peers seemed to support that the play was fine to perform. What do you believe could have happened differently in this scenario?
- Some texts have strict guidelines around changing language and lines. How might this have informed the decisions to select this play? How might this have been resolved if at all?

Case 12.3: Neurodiversity and Staffing

Beginning with the global COVID-19 pandemic, many companies, schools, and organizations pivoted from in person work to online practices. Many organizations quickly found themselves at a technology deficit as they tried to provide greater equity and access to technology, Wi-Fi, and equipment to their students and employees. At East State University, funds were allocated to hire additional technology support specialists to keep up with the growing demand to provide academic and user support.

Malcolm was hired at East State University during this time and was mostly responsible for answering online tickets or requests. He worked from home and was able to problem-solve via emails or the online chat function. To be hired for this position, Malcolm answered a standard online questionnaire, engaged in a brief interview with a supervisor, and passed a few simulation exercises that were conducted online. His answers were clear, direct, and to the point – a benefit when trying to help people navigate challenging and confusing problems.

After two years of online support, the school began to shift back to in person work requirements. There was significant pushback across different sectors – faculty, administrators, assistants, and support specialists – but the Board and Senior Team received pressure from tuition-paying families to either return back to in-person learning or risk losing significant enrollment.

Despite Malcolm's success engaging in online work, the IT department began to transition back to in-person support as the number of employees returned back to campus. Malcolm argued that most of his work was already done online and that he demonstrated his success in doing so. His supervisor said that Malcolm needed to work in person because that is what the entire university is doing.

On the first day back in person, Malcolm was anxious. He recognized the faces of his colleagues, since they had spent so much time online together, but he felt very disconnected from them. Some reached out to shake Malcolm's hand when they saw him but, uncomfortable with contact, Malcolm turned his body away from his colleague. His colleagues were not expecting this type of response. Moments later, his supervisor greeted him and showed him to his workstation.

After settling in, Malcolm put on noise-canceling headphones and logged into the computer. Colleagues were excited to see him in person and approached him. Each time, Malcolm focused on his screen, tightened the band on his headphones, and did not look up. After an hour, the supervisor called everyone to a staff meeting. Malcolm kept his headphones on, got up from his chair, moved to the conference room, and sat near the door.

As a way to welcome back the department, the supervisor asked for people to share their names and something they are looking forward to about being back in the office. People shared that it was nice to see colleagues face to face. Others shared it was nice to have some down time just to connect with others. Still others said it was nice to get out of the house. When it was Malcolm's turn, he responded, "Nothing. I want to be back at home." His colleagues laughed, thinking Malcolm was joking, but his face conveyed just how serious he was.

At the end of the day, the supervisor checked in with Malcolm and asked how his day was. Malcolm replied, "Fine, but I don't like being here." The supervisor is aware that returning to in-person work is an adjustment, but he was not expecting Malcolm to react so strongly to being in the office. He is beginning to wonder if this is the right team for Malcolm.

Identity-Conscious Reflection Questions (to be done on your own and/or in group)
- What issues of identity do you notice in this scenario? What is it about your own identities and experiences that made you notice these issues?
- What identities in this scenario do you feel connected to? What identities in this scenario do you feel disconnected or distanced from?

Identity-Conscious Framework (to be discussed as a group)
- Name it: What are the problems or challenges in this scenario that are impacted by identity?
- Own it: Where do these problems or challenges come from? What are the possible reasons that these issues related to identity are emerging?
- Interrupt it: Centering the experiences of identity, what could occur to address barriers, worries, fears, or hesitations in this scenario? What steps could be taken to remedy the issues?
- Take responsibility: What is the follow up to this situation? What might have occurred differently if the people in the scenario were centering identity-consciousness?

Identity-Conscious Discussion Questions (to be discussed as a group)
- What did you notice about your group's process in talking about this case study? How might the identity of your group inform and impact your approach to this case study?

Additional Points to Consider
- Transitions back to work in person were challenging for many people.
- While individuals might have to rely on their own capacity for adjustment, what could departments or supervisors have done to ease transitions?
- Who decides the institutional benefits of work schedules and arrangements (i.e. in-person vs remote)? Who does not get to decide or be a part of the decision making process?
- Without explicit disclosure, what might an individual who identifies with living with neurodivergence do to shape transition to a workplace?
- Is there a role for disclosure related to neurodivergence? What are the benefits of not disclosing? What are the challenges of not disclosing?

Case 12.4: The Assessment

You and your team have been asked to provide an initial classroom behavior assessment for a student you believe might benefit from psychoeducational testing. The child is a student of color who has been at the school for two years. In this first step, you are asked to complete a checklist of items related to observable behaviors. Each member of your grade-level team completes the checklist on their own and comes together to discuss the findings. You complete your checklist based on the observable behaviors in your classroom for this student that ask you to evaluate behaviors such as class participation, behavior during transition times, completing assignments on time, social interactions with peers, and ability to stay on task and focus. You respond honestly based on your experiences in class.

When you get together with the team and discuss your findings, you realize that your results are very different from the other members of your team. Your findings, however, do align most closely with the teacher of color. You have been engaging in identity-conscious work and wonder if your observations are rooted in particular racialized responses. You begin to wonder this in your meeting and say aloud, "I just want to name a dynamic that I'd like for us to discuss. I'm noticing that those who identify as people of color are reporting very different behaviors than those who identify as white, and I'd like for us to have a courageous conversation about this."

Your white colleagues look surprised and one of them replies, "What are you implying? We know from research that students of color are disproportionately referred for special education services. So, we don't see his behavior as a deficit. Maybe you and the other teacher are being too harsh with this student. Maybe you should ask yourself if you are stereotyping him based on race."

You feel your face get red and suddenly are embarrassed. Were you contributing to the overrepresentation of students of color being referred to special education? You begin to question whether or not you should even have this conversation with your team.

Identity-Conscious Reflection Questions (to be done on your own and/or in group)

- What issues of identity do you notice in this scenario? What is it about your own identities and experiences that made you notice these issues?
- What identities in this scenario do you feel connected to? What identities in this scenario do you feel disconnected or distanced from?

Identity-Conscious Framework (to be discussed as a group)

- Name it: What are the problems or challenges in this scenario that are impacted by identity?
- Own it: Where do these problems or challenges come from? What are the possible reasons that these issues related to identity are emerging?
- Interrupt it: Centering the experiences of identity, what could occur to address barriers, worries, fears, or hesitations in this scenario? What steps could be taken to remedy the issues?
- Take responsibility: What is the follow up to this situation? What might have occurred differently if the people in the scenario were centering identity-consciousness?

Identity-Conscious Discussion Questions (to be discussed as a group)

- What did you notice about your group's process in talking about this case study? How might the identity of your group inform and impact your approach to this case study?

Additional Points to Consider

- Students of color are disproportionately referred to special education (Ferri and Connor, 2005; Harry and Klinger, 2020).
- Students who need support should receive support.
- How might the teachers talk about this experience related to race?
- What might the teacher who brought up the issue do to address the feelings of embarrassment?
- How true could it be that the teachers of color saw something different than the white teachers on the team?

Case 12.5: Increased Stress

As Dean of Students at a private school, you are primarily responsible for the advising system, discipline, follow-up, and behavior improvement plans. Amy, a new 9th grader to the school, came with a very strong academic record and potential to be a competitive athlete on the varsity softball team. Amy is coming from a public school and, like many students making this transition from public to private, is struggling in the first few weeks. The pace of work is much faster than in Amy's previous school, and there is so much new material that Amy had never been taught.

Amy was sent to your office today because, as the teacher described, "Amy couldn't sit still, was making faces at me, and had repeated outbursts of humming. I kept telling Amy to stop, but she insisted she could not." In your meeting, Amy disclosed that she is living with Tourette Syndrome which can present itself more visibly when she is experiencing high levels of stress. Amy believes this change in environment, adjusting to new learning styles, and meeting so many new people has raised her stress level. Amy continued, "And, just so you are aware, if it really escalates, sometimes my Tourette Syndrome means I might say things that aren't quite appropriate at school. I just don't want to get in trouble for things that I can't control. And when I try to control it, honestly, it just makes it worse."

You have not met a student who lives with Tourette Syndrome (TS) and you don't believe that the school has enrolled any students with TS.

Identity-Conscious Reflection Questions (to be done on your own and/or in group)

- What issues of identity do you notice in this scenario? What is it about your own identities and experiences that made you notice these issues?
- What identities in this scenario do you feel connected to? What identities in this scenario do you feel disconnected or distanced from?

Identity-Conscious Framework (to be discussed as a group)

- Name it: What are the problems or challenges in this scenario that are impacted by identity?
- Own it: Where do these problems or challenges come from? What are the possible reasons that these issues related to identity are emerging?
- Interrupt it: Centering the experiences of identity, what could occur to address barriers, worries, fears, or hesitations in this scenario? What steps could be taken to remedy the issues?
- Take responsibility: What is the follow up to this situation? What might have occurred differently if the people in the scenario were centering identity-consciousness?

Identity-Conscious Discussion Questions (to be discussed as a group)

- What did you notice about your group's process in talking about this case study? How might the identity of your group inform and impact your approach to this case study?

Additional Points to Consider

- Tourette Syndrome (TS), also known as Tourette's Disorder: 1) At least 2 motor tics and at least 1 vocal (phonic) tic have been present, not necessarily at the same time. 2) Tics may wax and wane in frequency but have occurred for more than 1 year. 3) Tics started to appear before the age of 18. 4) Tics are not caused by the use of a substance or other medical condition (https://tourette.org/about-tourette/overview/what-is-tourette/).
- Teens living with TS may try to suppress and/or mask symptoms due to a desire to 'fit in' and be accepted by peers. How might the school create structures to support these transitions for Amy and other students?
- What aspects of professional development might need to be provided at the school? At what point do you bring in Amy and Amy's family?

13

Case Studies on Sexual Orientation

Chapter at a Glance

This chapter presents five case studies related to sexual orientation. Readers are encouraged to review the case study, engage in reflective practice using the guided questions provided, and participate in peer learning communities for dialogue. The goal is not to solve the case but rather practice slowing down, using an identity-conscious lens, and creating action for future use.

Case 13.1: The First

The Dizon School is a private school in a major metropolitan area. While there are many competing schools in the area, Dizon is known for being the most socially conservative of all the schools. During a time when many schools have shifted to being more inclusive of LGBTQ+ issues, race and racial justice, and addressing issues of inequity, Dizon has decided that they are going to stay true to their mission and values and keep with their existing curriculum. The Head of School, Board of Trustees, and Administrative team were relieved that they were not going to give in to the pressure of changing who they were. The school has also received full support from the parent community because they do not want academic rigor to be distracted by social justice pressures.

One of the strengths of The Dizon School is that they have one of the best performance arts programs in the local area. They have committed funds to hiring the best vocal teachers, acting coaches, and choreographers. Students are required to take a robust curriculum in the arts to graduate. And many choose Dizon because of this program.

In the past, via the admission cycle, there have been families where the parents identify as lesbian or gay. However, after the first few information sessions and meetings, many of these families withdraw their applications. Because of Dizon's socially conservative community and stated desire to not get involved in the current wave of "DEI and woke" movements, many families quickly come to the conclusion that they will not feel included or, worse, be targeted with bullying.

The Miller family decided they were going to apply to The Dizon School given their child's strong desire to pursue a career in performing arts. They are aware of the reputation of Dizon as preparing well-rounded actors, and are willing to explore further options for being in the community. In the first admissions meeting, the Millers met with Marilyn, the director. Marilyn was excited about their application and believed their child would be a great fit in the performing arts. "However," Marilyn continued. "I need you to know that this is not the most welcoming community for families with gay parents. While we are not a religiously affiliated school, many of our families are very socially and religiously conservative and often talk about homosexuality as being sinful. While we at Dizon discourage bullying, we know this does occur. If you continue in this application, I just want you to know that this might not be a family community that is kind. And, because of this, we have many young people who also believe the same thing. Why don't you think about it and let me know if you want to continue with the process?"

The Millers, already anticipating this conversation, agreed to proceed with the admissions process. They have faced adversity in their own lives, and they are well prepared to support their child in this community if they are accepted to the program. In a follow-up email, Marilyn wrote, "I am excited that you are continuing in the process. And, again, I want to reiterate, this may not be the most welcoming community to your type of family. If you were to enroll here, you would be the first LGBTQ+ family to stay."

Identity-Conscious Reflection Questions (to be done on your own and/or in group)

- What issues of identity do you notice in this scenario? What is it about your own identities and experiences that made you notice these issues?
- What identities in this scenario do you feel connected to? What identities in this scenario do you feel disconnected or distanced from?

Identity-Conscious Framework (to be discussed as a group)

- Name it: What are the problems or challenges in this scenario that are impacted by identity?
- Own it: Where do these problems or challenges come from? What are the possible reasons that these issues related to identity are emerging?
- Interrupt it: Centering the experiences of identity, what could occur to address barriers, worries, fears, or hesitations in this scenario? What steps could be taken to remedy the issues?
- Take responsibility: What is the follow up to this situation? What might have occurred differently if the people in the scenario were centering identity-consciousness?

Identity-Conscious Discussion Questions (to be discussed as a group)

- What did you notice about your group's process in talking about this case study? How might the identity of your group inform and impact your approach to this case study?

Additional Points to Consider

- What priorities come to mind as you read this scenario (e.g., strong arts department, inclusive community)?
- What might the Millers mean that they are well prepared to support their child if they were to go to The Dizon School?
- What assumptions might Marilyn be making about the community?
- How might Marilyn's role be informing and impacting family experiences in the process?
- What might the Millers ask others about the community? About the arts program?

Case 13.2: Isolation

Gina is an 11th grader who recently came out to her family. She was not surprised at how supportive they were given her family's vocal commitment to LGBTQ+ issues. But Gina's friend group and school climate is not very welcoming. In fact, very few people assume Gina to be gay because she is often seen with Mark, a classmate. They are together so much that teachers say, "Hey! You two! Stop flirting!" or "Gina and Mark, couple of the year." People believing that Mark is her partner and that the school is not very open to LGBTQ+ people makes it difficult to actually know who else might be gay and who might be interested in her.

Gina heard about a local gathering that was hosted by a youth LGBTQ+ organization a few towns over. Gina's parents dropped her off and made the remark, "We're sure you'll find someone who could be a great girlfriend there!" While Gina's parents try to be supportive, Gina was annoyed and said, "So, you just think all lesbians like each other?"

Being at the youth event, Gina learned that there were other kids who also were not out at school. One girl said, "I was even nervous about coming here in case I ran into someone who went to my school and would tell people I am gay." Gina reminded the new friend, "But… if they are here too…?"

The next day at school, Gina realized how different it felt being at the youth event and how she felt at school. School suddenly felt lonely and isolating. School felt small and unwelcoming. School felt like a place where she had to hide who she really is. Gina wants to start an LGBTQ+ group at school but is worried that this will not be received well by students or by teachers. She is confident there has to be other LGBTQ+ students, even at this small school, but she is not sure how to find others in her community.

Identity-Conscious Reflection Questions (to be done on your own and/or in group)

- What issues of identity do you notice in this scenario? What is it about your own identities and experiences that made you notice these issues?
- What identities in this scenario do you feel connected to? What identities in this scenario do you feel disconnected or distanced from?

Identity-Conscious Framework (to be discussed as a group)

- Name it: What are the problems or challenges in this scenario that are impacted by identity?
- Own it: Where do these problems or challenges come from? What are the possible reasons that these issues related to identity are emerging?
- Interrupt it: Centering the experiences of identity, what could occur to address barriers, worries, fears, or hesitations in this scenario? What steps could be taken to remedy the issues?
- Take responsibility: What is the follow up to this situation? What might have occurred differently if the people in the scenario were centering identity-consciousness?

> **Identity-Conscious Discussion Questions (to be discussed as a group)**
> - What did you notice about your group's process in talking about this case study? How might the identity of your group inform and impact your approach to this case study?
>
> **Additional Points to Consider**
> - What do you think Gina noticed as different at the youth event?
> - What experiences at your school might feel isolating and unwelcoming?
> - What risks do you believe Gina would have to take to make this group a reality?
> - What conflicts or risks might arise as Gina explores the possibility of a group?

Case 13.3: Everyone Says It

Holmes High School is a large, public, urban school with over 2,500 students. The demographics of the student body is very diverse, representing different socioeconomic statuses, racial and ethnic groups, religions, and languages. While it may seem that the diversity brings with it heightened sensitivity and respect, the school culture is such that "anything goes" in terms of how people talk to one another. For example, it is not uncommon to hear Black students using the "n-word" toward each other or hearing language that references socioeconomic status, such as "ghetto" or "hood."

Andre Jones is a new teacher at Holmes High who identifies as white and gay. He has chosen to work in a school like Holmes because he grew tired of the privileged, wealthy, predominantly white school he had worked at for over a decade. Andre wanted to bring his experience to a community that had a teacher shortage and needed experienced educators to join the faculty.

Andre knows that it takes time to gain the respect of students in any new environment, and he has been really trying to connect with this new population and demographic for him. He has decided not to intervene when Black students use racial language with each other, despite the fact that it makes him uncomfortable in the classroom. However, the students have begun to use slurs that refer to the LGBTQ+ community. Andre does not believe the students know his sexual orientation, and he does not sense they are saying it to him. However, he has noticed that the students refer to each other as a put-down or an insult when they call each other these homophobic slurs. Later that day in the faculty room, Andre asked others if they have been hearing students use homophobic language. The faculty all responded, "Sure we do. Everyone says it here. There's nothing to do about it because it's pervasive."

Andre knows how important it is to build relationships in the classroom. He also does not want to disclose his own sexual orientation by personalizing this. Yet, each day that he comes to the classroom and hears these words, he feels less and less connected to the students. Andre has told himself he needs to say something because he believes there might be LGTBQ+ students in his classroom who are also hearing these words and watching him be silent.

Identity-Conscious Reflection Questions (to be done on your own and/or in group)
- What issues of identity do you notice in this scenario? What is it about your own identities and experiences that made you notice these issues?
- What identities in this scenario do you feel connected to? What identities in this scenario do you feel disconnected or distanced from?

Identity-Conscious Framework (to be discussed as a group)
- Name it: What are the problems or challenges in this scenario that are impacted by identity?
- Own it: Where do these problems or challenges come from? What are the possible reasons that these issues related to identity are emerging?
- Interrupt it: Centering the experiences of identity, what could occur to address barriers, worries, fears, or hesitations in this scenario? What steps could be taken to remedy the issues?
- Take responsibility: What is the follow up to this situation? What might have occurred differently if the people in the scenario were centering identity-consciousness?

Identity-Conscious Discussion Questions (to be discussed as a group)
- What did you notice about your group's process in talking about this case study? How might the identity of your group inform and impact your approach to this case study?

Additional Points to Consider

- What might the student reactions be if Mr. Jones says something?
- What assumptions does this case make about the people in this situation?
- Mr. Jones keeps emphasizing relationships - to what extent is the relationship an opportunity or a barrier?
- How might Mr. Jones's silence on other slurs inform or impact this scenario?

Case 13.4: Health Education

Anthony is a 10th grade student and is taking a required health education class at school. Mrs. Matthews, a middle-aged white woman, has been teaching the class for over fifteen years. When Mrs. Matthews began teaching the class, the textbook mostly talked about health and sexuality through the lens of heterosexual frameworks. The textbook uses language such as "the purpose of intercourse is for pregnancy" and uses examples of sex and intercourse from a heterosexual – one man and one woman – perspective. In the chapter on contraception, the textbook talks about the use of condoms for the prevention of pregnancy and does not include information about sexually transmitted diseases that can be passed on in other types of intercourse.

At the start of the school year, all of the teachers are asked to submit draft versions of their lesson plans to the department chair. Because Mrs. Matthews had been teaching this same class for many years, she submitted her previous course guide. Her department chair knows she has had glowing reviews in the past and does not check on her or her teaching.

As Mrs. Matthews was beginning the chapter on sex and health, she decided to supplement lessons from the book with those she found from reputable LGBTQ+ sources on the internet. These sources disrupted the language of men/women as the only intercourse pairing and instead included men/men and women/women as well as including people who identify as transgender and non-binary. She no longer taught the chapter that simply stated condoms were to prevent pregnancy and instead included how LGBTQ+ communities can engage in safer sex. At the end of class one day, Mrs. Matthews found a note on her desk that simply said, "Thank you. From, Anthony."

At the end of the week, Mrs. Matthews was asked to meet with the department chair who had heard some students talking about the class over lunch. He checked the submitted course guide and there were no references to the new material Mrs. Matthews was teaching. He had not heard from any parents but was sure there were going to be phone calls and emails from them soon.

Identity-Conscious Reflection Questions (to be done on your own and/or in group)

- What issues of identity do you notice in this scenario? What is it about your own identities and experiences that made you notice these issues?
- What identities in this scenario do you feel connected to? What identities in this scenario do you feel disconnected or distanced from?

Identity-Conscious Framework (to be discussed as a group)

- Name it: What are the problems or challenges in this scenario that are impacted by identity?
- Own it: Where do these problems or challenges come from? What are the possible reasons that these issues related to identity are emerging?
- Interrupt it: Centering the experiences of identity, what could occur to address barriers, worries, fears, or hesitations in this scenario? What steps could be taken to remedy the issues?
- Take responsibility: What is the follow up to this situation? What might have occurred differently if the people in the scenario were centering identity-consciousness?

Identity-Conscious Discussion Questions (to be discussed as a group)

- What did you notice about your group's process in talking about this case study? How might the identity of your group inform and impact your approach to this case study?

Key Points to Consider

- What is the responsibility of sex and health educators as they talk about heterosexual and other relationships?
- Is Anthony's age relevant here as a 10th grader?
- What does the department chair anticipate as a result of Mrs. Matthews's new content?
- How might the textbook serve as a barrier to the work? What steps could be taken to remedy this barrier? What conflicts or risks might arise?
- What, if any, is the role of the school administrators in this case study?

Case 13.5: Waiting to Respond

Ann is the Director of Multicultural Affairs at a small, private Catholic college. She reports to the Vice President for Student Affairs. The college does not have a separate Gender and Sexuality Center, so much of the work related to gender and sexual orientation falls under Ann's responsibilities.

In the national news, there has been an increase in reported violence against members of the LGBTQ+ community. While there is not a significant presence of LGBTQ+ students at this Catholic college, there are many allies who are socially active and believe in amplifying the voices of LGBTQ+ communities. As a result of the number of incidents reported in the country, the students organized a demonstration during lunch called a "Die-In" where they wore black, wrote the names of LGBTQ+ people who have died as a result of violence, and lay on the ground in front of the student center. The college also has an active Communications and Journalism major, and a number of students took photos and wrote up reports of the event. Because of this, the event drew the attention of local media who reported on the Die-In.

Publicly supporting LGBTQ+ issues is tricky at this Catholic college. There has been a conservative approach to issues of sexual orientation and the college has withheld openly supporting identity and affinity groups. Yet, there are certainly LGBTQ+ students at the college. The students who organized the Die-In, while affiliated with the office Ann oversees, did not do it on behalf of the office. They were motivated to create awareness and draw attention to how important it is to create an inclusive community for all.

That evening, Ann got a call from the Vice President of Student Affairs who was angry about that afternoon's demonstration. Ann assumed the VP was upset because it caused a disruption at the entrance of the student center. Instead, the VP said, "You should have waited and gotten other offices to join you. Because you were not collaborative, your office is getting all the credit. That left out lots of others offices who could have joined like Community Services or Student Activities or Resident Assistants. Because they weren't involved, it looks like they don't care. With only your office's name attached, it looks like only your office cares about these issues. What you did was very selfish."

Ann was confused. Was the VP saying that Ann should have waited to be more collaborative and had a greater impact, or was the VP saying that Ann acted selfishly for having it only be students supported by the center? The VP ended with, "I expect next time you will not rush into these things and think about who else you can include in these activities."

Identity-Conscious Reflection Questions (to be done on your own and/or in group)

- What issues of identity do you notice in this scenario? What is it about your own identities and experiences that made you notice these issues?
- What identities in this scenario do you feel connected to? What identities in this scenario do you feel disconnected or distanced from?

Identity-Conscious Framework (to be discussed as a group)

- Name it: What are the problems or challenges in this scenario that are impacted by identity?
- Own it: Where do these problems or challenges come from? What are the possible reasons that these issues related to identity are emerging?
- Interrupt it: Centering the experiences of identity, what could occur to address barriers, worries, fears, or hesitations in this scenario? What steps could be taken to remedy the issues?
- Take responsibility: What is the follow up to this situation? What might have occurred differently if the people in the scenario were centering identity-consciousness?

Identity-Conscious Discussion Questions (to be discussed as a group)

- What did you notice about your group's process in talking about this case study? How might the identity of your group inform and impact your approach to this case study?

Key Points to Consider

- What do you believe was the Vice President's motive in this scenario? Where might the angry phone call be coming from?
- What do you believe was Ann's role in this scenario? What do you believe Ann should have done differently, if anything?
- What environmental factors contributed to the students organizing the demonstration? What do you believe was the impact of students in the communications and journalism department writing about the event?

14

Case Studies on Gender and Gender Identity

Chapter at a Glance

This chapter presents five case studies related to gender and gender identity. Readers are encouraged to review the case study, engage in reflective practice using the guided questions provided, and participate in peer learning communities for dialogue. The goal is not to solve the case but rather practice slowing down, using an identity-conscious lens, and creating action for future use.

Case 14.1: A Girl on the Team

Jenna has played football with her family since she was a little girl. Growing up with three brothers and two sisters, Jenna's parents encouraged the kids to think outside of the box when it came to identity and experiences. For example, two of Jenna's brothers decided to take classical dance and enrolled in after-school dance classes. One of Jenna's sisters was interested in ice hockey, and her dad drove her to the neighboring state where there was a robust girls' ice hockey group. There was no girls or coed football team where they lived, so Jenna's parents often set up casual games with young people in the town for Jenna to get experience playing. She eventually excelled past the skill levels of the kids in the pick-up games and was seeking a more competitive opportunity.

DOI: 10.4324/9781003508489-18

When Jenna entered high school, she wanted to try out for the football team. She had heard of a few girls in other parts of the country who had made national news for playing on boys' teams, and she felt she deserved a chance to show the team what she could do. On the day of tryouts, Jenna suited up and proceeded onto the field. The coaching staff was confused, although they had heard rumors about Jenna coming to try out. They had not had a girl try out for the team in the past, and they were unsure what they needed to do. Do they tell the boys to "go easy" when facing Jenna? Do they tell Jenna's family that it's their liability if she gets hurt? The coaches, all who identified as men, did not know what to do.

On that day, they decided to just let Jenna experience tryouts like any of the players. They did not give any special speeches or draw attention to Jenna. They required her to run the same drills as every other player and to hold Jenna to the same rubric of evaluation for tryouts. She consistently ran in the top 10% of the candidates, threw as far as many of the top players, and was as physically fit as the rest. At the end of the tryouts, the coaches met to talk about the players. They decided that Jenna certainly performed well. But, as a 9th grader, Jenna was not quite ready for the team. They believed that if she kept practicing, she could try out again next year.

Upon hearing the news that Jenna did not make the team, her family was upset and emailed the Athletic Director and the Principal stating they were seeking legal action against the Athletic department, the school, and the district for gender discrimination. The team does not believe they are in violation of Title IX but worry that this negative attention could impact how people view and support the athletic teams moving forward.

Identity-Conscious Reflection Questions (to be done on your own and/or in group)

- What issues of identity do you notice in this scenario? What is it about your own identities and experiences that made you notice these issues?
- What identities in this scenario do you feel connected to? What identities in this scenario do you feel disconnected or distanced from?

Identity-Conscious Framework (to be discussed as a group)

- Name it: What are the problems or challenges in this scenario that are impacted by identity?

- Own it: Where do these problems or challenges come from? What are the possible reasons that these issues related to identity are emerging?
- Interrupt it: Centering the experiences of identity, what could occur to address barriers, worries, fears, or hesitations in this scenario? What steps could be taken to remedy the issues?
- Take responsibility: What is the follow up to this situation? What might have occurred differently if the people in the scenario were centering identity-consciousness?

Identity-Conscious Discussion Questions (to be discussed as a group)
- What did you notice about your group's process in talking about this case study? How might the identity of your group inform and impact your approach to this case study?

Key Points to Consider
- Title IX requires that in sports where a girls team is not offered, girls must be allowed to try out for the boys' team and participate on the same basis as boys. What, beyond the legality of the situation, might the decision-makers want to pay attention to?
- Jenna's family individually provided support and encouragement for Jenna. What would an institutional response for support look like?
- The coaches were considering whether or not to say anything to the players about Jenna's participation in tryouts. They decided not to. What impact do you believe this had?

Case 14.2: Transitioning

The Tucker School is a grade 6–12 co-educational school just outside of a major city. While they have enjoyed a diverse community in terms of race, class, and sexual orientation, they have not had any faculty or students identify as transgender and transition while at the school.

A teacher who identified at the time as Ms. Eleanor Livingston is a teacher on the 9th grade team who has been at The Tucker School for three years. In October, Ms. Livingston approached the administrative team to let them know she identifies as transgender and had decided to begin the transition process from female to male next month. The teacher let the team know that he has already begun taking hormones and will have surgery over the December break. When the teacher returns, he will no longer use the name Eleanor but instead will use the name Ean, will use the honorific "Mr.", and use he/him pronouns.

The administrative team is unsure what to do. They have never had a member of the community, while at Tucker, identify as transgender. Individually and collectively, no one on the team has ever supervised or worked with someone who has transitioned. And, they are unsure what they are supposed to do as Mr. Livingston returns back to school in January. They begin to draft a list of things that would need to occur: letters home to families, an all-school assembly, options for families in Mr. Livingston's class to switch teachers, and a public statement in case the information hits the news cycle. They are fearful that people will say things like this will be too confusing for the students Mr. Livingston teaches and that they will not want their children being taught by Mr. Livingston.

One of the members of the administrative team says, "We need to brace ourselves for the worst-case scenario. This is going to be a public relations nightmare. What are we going to do?" Mr. Livingston's direct supervisor said, "I don't think this is going to be an issue at all. Mr. Livingston is an outstanding teacher, well respected among the faculty, and appreciated by students. It is our job to do whatever we can to make sure he can continue to be those things here at The Tucker School."

Identity-Conscious Reflection Questions (to be done on your own and/or in group)

- What issues of identity do you notice in this scenario? What is it about your own identities and experiences that made you notice these issues?
- What identities in this scenario do you feel connected to? What identities in this scenario do you feel disconnected or distanced from?

Identity-Conscious Framework (to be discussed as a group)

- Name it: What are the problems or challenges in this scenario that are impacted by identity?
- Own it: Where do these problems or challenges come from? What are the possible reasons that these issues related to identity are emerging?
- Interrupt it: Centering the experiences of identity, what could occur to address barriers, worries, fears, or hesitations in this scenario? What steps could be taken to remedy the issues?

- Take responsibility: What is the follow up to this situation? What might have occurred differently if the people in the scenario were centering identity-consciousness?

Identity-Conscious Discussion Questions (to be discussed as a group)
- What did you notice about your group's process in talking about this case study? How might the identity of your group inform and impact your approach to this case study?

Key Points to Consider
- What do you believe contributes to the administrative team's worry about "confusion of the students"?
- Do you believe there is anything Mr. Livingston needs to do before leaving for winter break in order to create a smooth transition in January?
- What should be a response to parents who may want to switch teachers?
- What other structural changes must be considered in order to support Mr. Livingston's return in January?

Case 14.3: Bathrooms and Access

Stewart High School is housed in an old 1950s-style building that has been renovated cosmetically over the years. In addition to basic accessibility (e.g., ramps, electric doors), there are needs to update bathrooms both from a physical accessibility lens and also a gender-inclusive lens. Currently, the majority of the bathrooms at Stewart High School are binary – men/women – and there are only three single-user bathrooms: 1) the Head of School office; 2) the Health/Nurse office; and 3) a bathroom at the basement level where there are no classrooms but mostly storage closets.

Over the years, there has been a growing number of students who identify as transgender and gender non-binary who have expressed that access to bathrooms has been an issue. While some continue to use binary-designated bathrooms (e.g., separate bathrooms for men and women), they have stated that having a single user bathroom or a gender-inclusive bathroom would make access easier. Some do use the bathroom in the nurse's office, but the bathroom in the basement near the storage rooms has not felt like a safe option for the students.

A group of students has asked to meet with the administrative team, including the Director of Facilities and the Chief Financial Officer, to see what can be done about the physical bathroom situation. Both administrators have echoed that it is impossible to change the bathrooms because of code requirements and the cost associated with having to renovate these areas. The students anticipated this response and turned to the Head of School, Dean of Students, and Upper School principal and asked, "Well, knowing that the physical bathrooms cannot change, what plans do you have for shifting the culture at this school for making it safer to be transgender or non-binary? What are your plans for making bathroom access safer for students?" One of the students added, "I don't think you understand what it's like for me as a non-binary student here. Not only do I feel afraid going into the bathrooms, it is actually unsafe to go into them because of how I look and how others perceive me."

Identity-Conscious Reflection Questions (to be done on your own and/or in group)

- What issues of identity do you notice in this scenario? What is it about your own identities and experiences that made you notice these issues?
- What identities in this scenario do you feel connected to? What identities in this scenario do you feel disconnected or distanced from?

Identity-Conscious Framework (to be discussed as a group)

- Name it: What are the problems or challenges in this scenario that are impacted by identity?
- Own it: Where do these problems or challenges come from? What are the possible reasons that these issues related to identity are emerging?
- Interrupt it: Centering the experiences of identity, what could occur to address barriers, worries, fears, or hesitations in this scenario? What steps could be taken to remedy the issues?
- Take responsibility: What is the follow up to this situation? What might have occurred differently if the people in the scenario were centering identity-consciousness?

Identity-Conscious Discussion Questions (to be discussed as a group)

- What did you notice about your group's process in talking about this case study? How might the identity of your group inform and impact your approach to this case study?

> **Key Points to Consider**
> - While the administrators were focused on the building structure, the students were encouraging dialogue about the culture and climate of the school. What are possible responses from the administrative team?
> - What solutions have you seen at your schools to address bathrooms, access, climate, and safety?
> - If renovating the facilities is not possible, what other possibilities can exist to create a more inclusive and accessible process?

Case 14.4: The Group Project

You teach a project-based course in the upper division where students complete eight (8) group projects throughout the year. On the first project, the students get to choose their own groups. You are not surprised that the groups are divided across gender lines: boys are with boys and girls are with girls. The students go off to the library to do their research, use class time to discuss their projects and work on their papers or presentations, and present to the class two weeks later. In between classes, students are working on these projects at home and bringing in their research during the next class.

The second time around, you assign students new topics and new groups. There happens to be fewer girls than boys in the class, so you create groups of four boys and a girl. The schedule is the same – they are assigned their projects, conduct research in the library, work during class time on their assignments, and present to the class. The presentations are once again successful. This cycle repeats itself another two times with new group assignments. Still, there tends to be one girl in the group and a number of boys.

During a free period, the girls from your class ask if they can use your classroom to hang out and relax. You are in the room planning for the next sequence of projects.

You overhear the girls talking about how annoying the boys are in the class. They ask each other how it's going with the group projects and every single girl responds, "I hate it. I'm the one who has to do all the work while the boys just sit around and wait for directions." As the teacher, you say, "I'm sorry to interrupt you all. But did I hear you correctly – the boys aren't really pulling their weight in the group projects?" The students respond, "Yes, why don't you know that? All they do is wait for one of us girls to tell them what to do. And, even when we assign roles and give them their work, they do it totally halfway. So, we end up having to do all the work for the boys in the group and our own work!" You respond, "That's happening with all of you girls?" They respond in unison, "Yes!"

You wonder what is going on in these groups. You thought it was a good idea to make sure there was gender diversity in the groups by having at least one girl in the project groups. But, you also realize you only leave one girl in any group. You wonder if you've sent some sort of message about how work is divided or who does the labor. Maybe you weren't clear enough that this was a group project? Or, is there something going on related to gender, roles, and expectations here?

Identity-Conscious Reflection Questions (to be done on your own and/or in group)
- What issues of identity do you notice in this scenario? What is it about your own identities and experiences that made you notice these issues?
- What identities in this scenario do you feel connected to? What identities in this scenario do you feel disconnected or distanced from?

Identity-Conscious Framework (to be discussed as a group)
- Name it: What are the problems or challenges in this scenario that are impacted by identity?
- Own it: Where do these problems or challenges come from? What are the possible reasons that these issues related to identity are emerging?
- Interrupt it: Centering the experiences of identity, what could occur to address barriers, worries, fears, or hesitations in this scenario? What steps could be taken to remedy the issues?
- Take responsibility: What is the follow up to this situation? What might have occurred differently if the people in the scenario were centering identity-consciousness?

Identity-Conscious Discussion Questions (to be discussed as a group)
- What did you notice about your group's process in talking about this case study? How might the identity of your group inform and impact your approach to this case study?

Key Points to Consider
- While it may seem the girls are engaging in leadership roles, what is the dynamic that is occurring in these situations?
- How might this situation be hurting the boys? What might they be learning as a result of these behaviors?
- What options does the teacher have in this scenario to address issues of gender?

Case 14.5: Disclosing Names and Pronouns

Iris is a 4th grader in a school that considers itself to be "progressive and liberal." Midway through the academic year, Iris approached her parents to tell them she "doesn't feel like a girl, but feels more like a boy." Iris's parents explained, in age-appropriate ways, language related to gender, gender identity, and pronouns. Iris, at the conclusion of that conversation, asked to be called "Ivan", and to use "he/him" pronouns.

The next morning, Ivan's parents called the school principal to set up a meeting to let the principal know about this decision. The principal thanked them for the information and said, "We will now work on a communication to go out to the entire school community letting everyone know about the change in name and that your child will be using different pronouns." Ivan's parents were surprised by the quick supportive nature of the conversation but grew concerned about a public community-wide statement. When asked about why there needed to be an all-school communication about the issue, the principal replied, "Well, it's only fair that other families know there is someone who might be transgender in the 4th grade so that they can be prepared." Ivan's parents replied, "We don't believe that this is necessary to send out an all school communication. In fact, by sending an all-school communication out, we believe you'll draw even more attention to Ivan. We believe you only need to notify his teachers so that they do not misgender him in class." The principal replied, "Unfortunately, I think this is the right way to go. Children will be going home saying that a girl is now a boy, and parents need to be prepared to receive those questions."

Ivan's parents left the meeting and were very uneasy about the direction of the conversation.

Identity-Conscious Reflection Questions (to be done on your own and/or in group)

- What issues of identity do you notice in this scenario? What is it about your own identities and experiences that made you notice these issues?
- What identities in this scenario do you feel connected to? What identities in this scenario do you feel disconnected or distanced from?

Identity-Conscious Framework (to be discussed as a group)

- Name it: What are the problems or challenges in this scenario that are impacted by identity?

- Own it: Where do these problems or challenges come from? What are the possible reasons that these issues related to identity are emerging?
- Interrupt it: Centering the experiences of identity, what could occur to address barriers, worries, fears, or hesitations in this scenario? What steps could be taken to remedy the issues?
- Take responsibility: What is the follow up to this situation? What might have occurred differently if the people in the scenario were centering identity-consciousness?

Identity-Conscious Discussion Questions (to be discussed as a group)
- What did you notice about your group's process in talking about this case study? How might the identity of your group inform and impact your approach to this case study?

Key Points to Consider
- What is the impact of the school self-identifying as "progressive and liberal" in this scenario?
- Why do you believe the leader's strategy was to tell the entire school about Ivan? How might conflict and risk have been a part of the reaction and decision?

15

Case Studies on Language

Chapter at a Glance

This chapter presents five case studies related to language and words. Readers are encouraged to review the case study, engage in reflective practice using the guided questions provided, and participate in peer learning communities for dialogue. The goal is not to solve the case but rather practice slowing down, using an identity-conscious lens, and creating action for future use.

Case 15.1: A Way to Connect

Miranda is an 8th grade teacher in a predominantly Black middle school. She is well liked by the students and enjoys her job. She prides herself on connecting with the students, meeting them where they are at, and being seen as relatable. During passing periods in between classes, Miranda stands in the hallway outside of her classroom door interacting with the students. As students walk away, she is often heard yelling down the hallway, "Have a great rest of your day! You are amazing! Love you!"

Joniece is a new teacher at the school and has heard Miranda say "I love you" to students. It has made her uncomfortable for a few reasons: 1) she sees that Miranda has a positive impact on the students and doesn't want to cause trouble; 2) she has overheard a few students say "I hate when she says that to me" as they have walked away from Miranda; and 3) Joniece feels as if there

DOI: 10.4324/9781003508489-19

is an underlying issue of race as Miranda is a white woman saying "Love you" to a group of young, Black teenagers.

Joniece decided to engage in a courageous conversation with Miranda, and Miranda was enthusiastic to talk with Joniece. When Joniece told Miranda the aspects of her discomfort, Miranda responded, "Well, I know that these kids don't hear the words 'love you' a lot at home, and I wanted to make sure they at least heard it once a day. So, I don't mind being seen as inappropriate as long as I'm doing something positive for the kids!"

Identity-Conscious Reflection Questions (to be done on your own and/or in group):

- What issues of identity do you notice in this scenario? What is it about your own identities and experiences that made you notice these issues?
- What identities in this scenario do you feel connected to? What identities in this scenario do you feel disconnected or distanced from?

Identity-Conscious Framework (to be discussed as a group)

- Name it: What are the problems or challenges in this scenario that are impacted by identity?
- Own it: Where do these problems or challenges come from? What are the possible reasons that these issues related to identity are emerging?
- Interrupt it: Centering the experiences of identity, what could occur to address barriers, worries, fears, or hesitations in this scenario? What steps could be taken to remedy the issues?
- Take responsibility: What is the follow up to this situation? What might have occurred differently if the people in the scenario were centering identity-consciousness?

Identity-Conscious Discussion Questions (to be discussed as a group)

- What did you notice about your group's process in talking about this case study? How might the identity of your group inform and impact your approach to this case study?

Key Points to Consider

- What meaning do you make of Miranda's comment that some of the students don't hear the words "love you" in their homes?
- How might Miranda's identity as a white woman inform and impact Joniece's discomfort?

Case 15.2: The Email

You are the chair of a search committee in charge of hiring a classroom teacher for 7th grade. After multiple rounds, you have a candidate who has excelled in the search. He is early in his career, but he demonstrated a great deal of potential. You watched his sample lesson, observed him with students, and read his writing sample. You conducted a reference check and feel confident that this teacher is the right match for the team, the division, and for the leadership committee.

Later that evening, you open up your email box and see an email from the candidate. You excitedly click on the email, thinking this may be an email response accepting your offer. It starts by greeting you by name. You skim the first few lines of the email and see the name of your school in the body of the email. As you continued reading, however, you became a little confused. Though it is your email in the address line and your name in the greeting, the tone of the email seems unprofessional. The text is very informal and written with grammatical and spelling errors. There are some references to the people he met and some judgmental observations about them. Much of the email is written using slang phrases and there is no shortage of profanity. Only when you finish the email do you realize that, perhaps, the candidate mistakenly sent it to you and it was probably intended for a friend with a similar name and email as yours.

You think back to the actual interview and to the writing sample. Everything seems to check out, but this email is really bothering you. You are second-guessing whether or not this person really is the right candidate for the job.

Identity-Conscious Reflection Questions (to be done on your own and/or in group):

- What issues of identity do you notice in this scenario? What is it about your own identities and experiences that made you notice these issues?
- What identities in this scenario do you feel connected to? What identities in this scenario do you feel disconnected or distanced from?

Identity-Conscious Framework (to be discussed as a group)

- Name it: What are the problems or challenges in this scenario that are impacted by identity?

- Own it: Where do these problems or challenges come from? What are the possible reasons that these issues related to identity are emerging?
- Interrupt it: Centering the experiences of identity, what could occur to address barriers, worries, fears, or hesitations in this scenario? What steps could be taken to remedy the issues?
- Take responsibility: What is the follow up to this situation? What might have occurred differently if the people in the scenario were centering identity-consciousness?

Identity-Conscious Discussion Questions (to be discussed as a group)

- What did you notice about your group's process in talking about this case study? How might the identity of your group inform and impact your approach to this case study?

Key Points to Consider

- How might your own identity and experiences inform your processing of the email?
- Who might you consider sharing this information with?
- What might you say to the candidate if you chose to address this email incident?
- Does the fact that this was intended for a friend change how you view the language in this email?

Case 15.3: Must Speak English

Mr. Gonzales – often referred to by staff and students as Miguel – has worked on the maintenance team for 15 years. He is the most senior member on the team and regularly goes above and beyond what is asked of him. The rest of the maintenance team is made up of men, like Miguel, who identify as Spanish-speaking. Miguel has a great relationship with the team. He has served as a mentor to members of the team and, on occasion, has helped to facilitate some meetings when the school needed nuanced information translated. When the maintenance team is together, they often speak Spanish.

Recently, the current Director of Facilities, who had only been in the role for three years, has decided to move out of state. When the position for the Director job was posted, Miguel met all of the qualifications. However, when he applied for the job, the Human Resources manager asked to speak with him. She wanted to tell him personally that he would likely not move forward in the role because the job required the Director to write, read, and communicate in English fluently. Miguel was taken aback by this comment given that he has lived in this country for twenty-five years and does speak English fluently, albeit with an accent. No one has ever complained that it was difficult to understand or communicate with Miguel.

"I'm curious," Miguel asked. "I see you have a requirement to speak English fluently, but why don't you have a requirement to speak Spanish fluently? After all, the entire team is Spanish-speaking, and a Director who only speaks English actually can't communicate as well to them. That's why you are always asking me to translate!"

"But the majority of whom you will be interacting and writing reports for speak, read, and write in English, Miguel," the HR Director stated.

Identity-Conscious Reflection Questions (to be done on your own and/or in group)

- What issues of identity do you notice in this scenario? What is it about your own identities and experiences that made you notice these issues?
- What identities in this scenario do you feel connected to? What identities in this scenario do you feel disconnected or distanced from?

Identity-Conscious Framework (to be discussed as a group)

- Name it: What are the problems or challenges in this scenario that are impacted by identity?
- Own it: Where do these problems or challenges come from? What are the possible reasons that these issues related to identity are emerging?
- Interrupt it: Centering the experiences of identity, what could occur to address barriers, worries, fears, or hesitations in this scenario? What steps could be taken to remedy the issues?
- Take responsibility: What is the follow up to this situation? What might have occurred differently if the people in the scenario were centering identity-consciousness?

Identity-Conscious Discussion Questions (to be discussed as a group)

- What did you notice about your group's process in talking about this case study? How might the identity of your group inform and impact your approach to this case study?

Key Points to Consider

- The Equal Employment Opportunity Commission (EEOC) says an English-only rule may violate civil rights laws unless the employer can show the rule is necessary for conducting business. Do you believe the Director of Facilities position needs to speak English fluently in order to conduct business?
- Who gets to decide what the threshold is for fluency? What might the HR Director need to understand, know, or consider in this case?
- Should the school add that an ability to speak Spanish be added to the job posting?
- What are the benefits of hiring an internal candidate like Miguel? What are the benefits of hiring external candidates?

Case 15.4: The Rubric

Elaine is a masters student in the education program. Elaine came to the United States after she graduated from college and began working at a local middle school where she has been for over five years. It is clear that Elaine comes to class having read the assignments and you have seen that she has pages of notes in her notebook. You have even seen her printed copies of the articles and there are markings all over the pages. Elaine is not the first to respond during class discussions but, when called on, she always has a thoughtful contribution.

Elaine's writing, however, needs work. Her sentence structures are choppy and, while she uses terminology from the articles, the concepts and ideas are not synthesized. Using your existing rubric, you initially mark Elaine's paper with a C+.

You return Elaine's work to her the following class, and it is clear she is disappointed. After class, she stays behind to talk with you. Elaine mentions that she does not feel confident in her written expression of English. While she does speak it enough to do her job as a teacher and advisor, the level of comprehension and writing in the masters program feels very challenging to her. She mentioned that she often writes her papers in her home language and then translates them to English. You suggest she go to the writing center, only to realize how difficult it is to get to the writing center as someone who already works a full time day job.

Elaine has just turned in her second paper and, similar to the first, it needs a lot of work. You reflect on Elaine's statement that she writes her papers in her home language and then rewrites them in English. You wonder if your rubric accounts for this and whether your practice is inequitable. You also wonder if making accommodations for Elaine means lowering your standard of academic work in your class.

Identity-Conscious Reflection Questions (to be done on your own and/or in group):

- What issues of identity do you notice in this scenario? What is it about your own identities and experiences that made you notice these issues?
- What identities in this scenario do you feel connected to? What identities in this scenario do you feel disconnected or distanced from?

Identity-Conscious Framework (to be discussed as a group)

- Name it: What are the problems or challenges in this scenario that are impacted by identity?
- Own it: Where do these problems or challenges come from? What are the possible reasons that these issues related to identity are emerging?
- Interrupt it: Centering the experiences of identity, what could occur to address barriers, worries, fears, or hesitations in this scenario? What steps could be taken to remedy the issues?
- Take responsibility: What is the follow up to this situation? What might have occurred differently if the people in the scenario were centering identity-consciousness?

Identity-Conscious Discussion Questions (to be discussed as a group)

- What did you notice about your group's process in talking about this case study? How might the identity of your group inform and impact your approach to this case study?

Key Points to Consider

- What are the challenges that you and your colleagues may have in grading students who are English Language Learners?
- What are some strategies or tools that you find particularly helpful in grading English Language Learner work?
- What options exist beyond letter grades in writing, discussion, and class assignments?
- Does the fact that Elaine is in a masters program – an advanced degree program – impact your decision?

Case 15.5: The Competition

There has been a long athletic rivalry between North Lawson High School and Xavier High School. One of the most heated competitions is the basketball game which brings big crowds to the gymnasium. Because of the demographics of the two towns, the majority of the fans on the North Lawson High School side of the gymnasium are Black and the fans on the Xavier High School side are white.

Like with many athletic contests, there is a component of "trash talking" on the court. Players instigate reactions from the opposing side. Mark is a player on the North Lawson High School team. While facing off against a player from Xavier High School, Mark heard the other player use the "n-word" towards him. Mark stayed focused on the game and did not let this comment distract him. It's not that he hadn't heard that word before – his all-Black friend group does use this word casually. He admits that the word is pretty common. However, Mark had not been called that word by anyone white. He wondered if he had heard the other player wrong, so he chose to stay focused on the game.

The game ended in a disappointing loss for North Lawson High School. After the game, Mark couldn't stop thinking about what the other player said to him. He knew that day would come, but he just could not believe it happened to him that night. The next day, Mark approached his coach and told him what happened. His coach told Mark that he would like to call the Athletic Director and the coach from the other team and address this issue. Mark agreed.

Later that day, Mark was asked to come back to the athletic office. His coach told him that he spoke with the Xavier administrators who said, "My players would never use that word. They would never call anyone that word. I have already called that player into my office and he denies ever using that word against your player."

"Well," Mark's coach stated, "Mark would never make something like this up. So, I believe you and your player owe Mark an apology."

The Xavier coach said, "We will not be doing that. Our player did not say it, and your player is just being a sore loser."

> **Identity-Conscious Reflection Questions (to be done on your own and/or in group)**
>
> ◆ What issues of identity do you notice in this scenario? What is it about your own identities and experiences that made you notice these issues?
> ◆ What identities in this scenario do you feel connected to? What identities in this scenario do you feel disconnected or distanced from?

Identity-Conscious Framework (to be discussed as a group)

- Name it: What are the problems or challenges in this scenario that are impacted by identity?
- Own it: Where do these problems or challenges come from? What are the possible reasons that these issues related to identity are emerging?
- Interrupt it: Centering the experiences of identity, what could occur to address barriers, worries, fears, or hesitations in this scenario? What steps could be taken to remedy the issues?
- Take responsibility: What is the follow up to this situation? What might have occurred differently if the people in the scenario were centering identity-consciousness?

Identity-Conscious Discussion Questions (to be discussed as a group)

- What did you notice about your group's process in talking about this case study? How might the identity of your group inform and impact your approach to this case study?

Key Points to Consider

- What is the role of fact-finding in this scenario?
- What follow-up actions should the Athletic Director, Coach, and school follow with Mark?
- What options are available if Xavier's administrators insist that there was no wrongdoing?

16

Case Studies on Age

Chapter at a Glance

This chapter presents five case studies related to age. Readers are encouraged to review the case study, engage in reflective practice using the guided questions provided, and participate in peer learning communities for dialogue. The goal is not to solve the case but rather practice slowing down, using an identity-conscious lens, and creating action for future use.

Case 16.1: Set in My Ways

Helen is a teacher at your school who has been on the faculty for 30 years. She has taught decades of children and there are a number of parents at the school who also had Helen when they were students. She is considered a beloved teacher and the keeper of many historical references, stories, and contexts.

Over the past few years, Helen has seen a number of administrators come and go. She takes pride in "being here longer than any administrator" and jokes that "she could do every job at the school because she has been around so long." People take Helen's words at school very seriously.

One recent hire at the school has been Elizabeth, a senior administrator responsible for professional development. While Elizabeth provides a general array of professional development experiences, she has focused almost exclusively on issues of equity and inclusion. She has crafted learning opportunities for faculty to evaluate their curriculum, to make changes to represent more diverse perspectives, and build habits and skills for difficult dialogues. With the permission of the Head of School, Elizabeth has made professional development workshops related to equity and inclusion a part of the evaluation process for each teacher. At the end of the academic year, teachers meet with their division heads to talk about their progress on their equity and inclusion goals and seek support for areas of growth.

When Helen met with her division head, she stated, "I'm not doing this DEI stuff. I've been teaching for over 35 years. If that's not professional enough, then I don't know what is." Many agree that Helen is a master teacher and has a wealth of knowledge to share; however, her lessons have not changed or kept up with the shifting demographics and approaches to pedagogy. In particular, her lessons do not include diverse perspectives, readings, or opportunities for young people to learn about people of color, LGBTQ+ people, or people with disabilities. Her work is largely rooted in white and male perspectives. Helen has been vocal about the fact that she is "retiring and doesn't want to spend these last few years changing something she knows works."

Helen's division head is not sure what to do. On one hand, Helen does bring a wealth of experience and has demonstrated high markings on her evaluations. On the other hand, Helen is staying at the school for a few more years, and the direction of the school has been changing.

Identity-Conscious Reflection Questions (to be done on your own and/or in group)

- What issues of identity do you notice in this scenario? What is it about your own identities and experiences that made you notice these issues?
- What identities in this scenario do you feel connected to? What identities in this scenario do you feel disconnected or distanced from?

Identity-Conscious Framework (to be discussed as a group)

- Name it: What are the problems or challenges in this scenario that are impacted by identity?
- Own it: Where do these problems or challenges come from? What are the possible reasons that these issues related to identity are emerging?
- Interrupt it: Centering the experiences of identity, what could occur to address barriers, worries, fears, or hesitations in this scenario? What steps could be taken to remedy the issues?

- Take responsibility: What is the follow up to this situation? What might have occurred differently if the people in the scenario were centering identity-consciousness?

Identity-Conscious Discussion Questions (to be discussed as a group)
- What did you notice about your group's process in talking about this case study? How might the identity of your group inform and impact your approach to this case study?

Key Points to Consider
- Helen's experience is considered a value to the school. Her teaching and views reflect the traditions and values of the school.
- What is the role of flexibility in this scenario?
- How might the value of reputation be impacting this scenario?
- How does one validate the experience that Helen brings and also affirm that the school is changing direction? How might validation get in the way of progress?

Case 16.2: A Word in the Meeting

Roger has been on the teaching faculty for the past 37 years and has the longest tenure of any faculty at the school. In addition to his teaching responsibilities, Roger has served as the varsity baseball coach for the past 27 years and as a Head Advisor for the senior class for the past 15 years. He is beloved among the students and families and well respected by his colleagues. Next year, Roger plans on retiring.

Knowing he is entering into his final year in this community, Roger has been leaning into some of the professional development that, frankly, he knows he should have paid attention to for years. However, he has decided this year is his last chance to dive into some learning. Roger expressed interest in doing more work related to DEI. He started the year by asking the DEI Director for different books he should read and opportunities to engage in peer learning communities. He has been open to learning and admits that some of the ideas related to DEI are confusing to him. He believes that inequity exists, but he is struggling in his learning journey. He feels very behind everyone else at the school and is nervous about speaking up and saying the wrong thing.

Roger has been regularly attending the peer learning groups along with a racially diverse group of faculty. He has been mostly quiet. Many of his peers have noticed that he does not say much. Some have believed his silence is because Roger is disengaged. Others believe Roger is uncomfortable trying on new ideas. Still others believe Roger is here just to check off a box of participation.

At one of the peer learning dialogues, the group was talking about two Black male students, senior captains of the baseball team, who were not getting along. It seems the tension was so evident between these two students that others were saying that they might end up in a physical altercation. Roger spoke up and said, "I have known these two students ever since they were in 6th grade. Their relationship goes through highs and lows together. This behavior is pretty typical for them. I've been their advisor and have heard them say that it's challenging being the only Black boys in the grade. And, I agree – being two colored boys in an all-white school must be so difficult and…." Before Roger could finish his sentence, Tamira, a Black faculty member, raised her voice and said, "Stop! You did not just call these boys 'colored'. Seriously? Why are you even here? How could you even use that word in a space like this?" Tamira grabbed her things and left the room. Roger turned to his peers and said, "I'm so sorry. I didn't mean it in any bad way. I'm getting used to using the right words – I'm an old guy trying to learn new things."

Identity-Conscious Reflection Questions (to be done on your own and/or in group):

- What issues of identity do you notice in this scenario? What is it about your own identities and experiences that made you notice these issues?
- What identities in this scenario do you feel connected to? What identities in this scenario do you feel disconnected or distanced from?

Identity-Conscious Framework (to be discussed as a group)

- Name it: What are the problems or challenges in this scenario that are impacted by identity?
- Own it: Where do these problems or challenges come from? What are the possible reasons that these issues related to identity are emerging?
- Interrupt it: Centering the experiences of identity, what could occur to address barriers, worries, fears, or hesitations in this scenario? What steps could be taken to remedy the issues?
- Take responsibility: What is the follow up to this situation? What might have occurred differently if the people in the scenario were centering identity-consciousness?

Identity-Conscious Discussion Questions (to be discussed as a group)

- What did you notice about your group's process in talking about this case study? How might the identity of your group inform and impact your approach to this case study?

Key Points to Consider

- To what extent does Roger's comment about age feel relevant to this scenario?
- Why do you believe Roger connected his age to the use of language?
- How might Roger's statement that he is retiring next year inform or impact his desire to engage in learning related to DEI?
- How might the dynamic in a peer learning group impact this scenario?
- What might others do to support Tamira? What connections might there be between identity and this response?

Case 16.3: A New Assistant Director

When Gracie was in high school, she was a four-season athlete, a student leader, and an admissions ambassador. She really enjoyed her time at Bautista Academy, particularly because of the mentorship and guidance she received from so many of her teachers, coaches, and administrators. She truly felt like she belonged at Bautista Academy and that the community saw her for all of her strengths and talents. Gracie was nervous about going to college and wondered if she'd find the same encouraging community that she had in high school.

In college, Gracie's world opened up in many different and unexpected ways. She took courses like Black Feminist Thought, Law and Society, Children of Color and Schools, and Anti-Racism in Education. Gracie had never thought about these issues prior to coming to college because she always felt like the faculty at Bautista Academy never treated her like she was different because she was Latinx. Issues of race and inequity never came up in her high school conversations. While she enjoyed taking these classes, she found herself questioning all that she experienced in high school. Looking back, Gracie began to remember comments that people made that, perhaps, were rooted in racism such as the time when her classmate said, "Of course they picked Gracie to be a leader – they needed more diversity" or when a teacher said, "You're such a strong student, especially given how hard you have to work to overcome things."

Upon graduation, Gracie noticed there was a teaching apprentice position at Bautista Academy. Gracie applied for the position and immediately was offered an interview at the school. The faculty on the interview committee were so happy to see her that they spent most of the time chatting with her about fond memories rather than asking her key interview questions. Soon after, Gracie was offered the position and started that August.

When Gracie pulled onto campus, she felt anxious – a feeling she had not felt in previous visits to campus. Gracie was looking at Bautista Academy with a different lens. Gracie noticed that she was feeling angry and resentful about her time there. She took a deep breath, walked in the front door, and sat down at the faculty orientation meeting. Gracie introduced herself to a new faculty member. Gracie mentioned that she was a graduate of Bautista, but that she intended on making lots of changes while she was here.

As the weeks went on and students arrived back to campus, Gracie saw her experiences differently than when she was a student. She grew agitated when faculty would talk about the "students who are having difficulty transitioning to Bautista" and noticed all the students listed here were students of color. She overheard students during lunch talking about their lavish summer vacations and how some students of color "probably just had to stay home." In advisory meetings, she heard faculty talk about behavior issues and lack of parent involvement, and noticed that all of the students and parents they were mentioning were Black.

Gracie couldn't take it anymore. She went back to the faculty office and sent an email to the entire faculty about how upset she was, how racist people's behaviors are at this school, and how she is surprised she even made it out of Bautista in one piece. Gracie listed all of the things that needed to change immediately and cited research from the classes she had taken while at college. She ended with, "And if these things don't change immediately, I'm going to make sure that every family of color knows what's actually going on here at Bautista Academy."

Identity-Conscious Reflection Questions (to be done on your own and/or in group):
- What issues of identity do you notice in this scenario? What is it about your own identities and experiences that made you notice these issues?
- What identities in this scenario do you feel connected to? What identities in this scenario do you feel disconnected or distanced from?

Identity-Conscious Framework (to be discussed as a group)

- Name it: What are the problems or challenges in this scenario that are impacted by identity?
- Own it: Where do these problems or challenges come from? What are the possible reasons that these issues related to identity are emerging?
- Interrupt it: Centering the experiences of identity, what could occur to address barriers, worries, fears, or hesitations in this scenario? What steps could be taken to remedy the issues?
- Take responsibility: What is the follow up to this situation? What might have occurred differently if the people in the scenario were centering identity-consciousness?

Identity-Conscious Discussion Questions (to be discussed as a group)

- What did you notice about your group's process in talking about this case study? How might the identity of your group inform and impact your approach to this case study?

Key Points to Consider

- What might support for Gracie look like in this scenario?
- How, if at all, might age be used as an excuse in this scenario?
- How, if at all, might age be dismissed in this scenario?
- What intersections might exist between identities in this scenario?
- What was the role of the interview team in this scenario?
- What opportunities exist in this scenario related to age and identity?

Case 16.4: The Parent Group

In her professional life, Maria made decisions about her career that advanced her quickly through the ranks at her institution. She focused on research and publishing, writing her first two books, and making a name for herself in the field. A few years after Maria earned academic tenure, a goal she had focused on for so many years, she decided she wanted to start a family. Now solidly in her mid-40s, Maria was not sure if she could have biological children, but she successfully became pregnant and delivered a beautiful and healthy baby.

Maria was excited when her child turned five and was of school age because she, herself, loved school and wanted her child to experience the same joys. On the first day of kindergarten orientation, Maria was nervous about meeting other parents but eager to make new friends. When Maria walked into the classroom, she immediately noticed a difference between herself and the other parents – the age difference from herself and what she perceived to be the ages of the other parents was a stark contrast. She had just turned fifty years old and, it appeared, that the average age of the parents in the room was late twenties.

The other parents all seemed to know each other based on their easy demeanor with one another and the quickness that their children started playing. Maria's child was still holding on to Maria's pant leg. When it was time for the orientation to begin, Maria's guess that the other parents knew each other was confirmed as they shared similar preschools their children had attended, their extracurricular activities, what teams they played on for sports, and where they took music lessons. Maria had not enrolled her child in any of those activities.

When orientation ended, Maria lingered to talk with the classroom teacher. She wanted some advice about how to best transition her child to the classroom given that she did not know other children. But, really, Maria wanted to know how she, herself, might best transition into the parent group that already seemed very exclusive.

Identity-Conscious Reflection Questions (to be done on your own and/or in group):

- What issues of identity do you notice in this scenario? What is it about your own identities and experiences that made you notice these issues?
- What identities in this scenario do you feel connected to? What identities in this scenario do you feel disconnected or distanced from?

Identity-Conscious Framework (to be discussed as a group)

- Name it: What are the problems or challenges in this scenario that are impacted by identity?
- Own it: Where do these problems or challenges come from? What are the possible reasons that these issues related to identity are emerging?
- Interrupt it: Centering the experiences of identity, what could occur to address barriers, worries, fears, or hesitations in this scenario? What steps could be taken to remedy the issues?
- Take responsibility: What is the follow up to this situation? What might have occurred differently if the people in the scenario were centering identity-consciousness?

Identity-Conscious Discussion Questions (to be discussed as a group)
- What did you notice about your group's process in talking about this case study? How might the identity of your group inform and impact your approach to this case study?

Key Points to Consider
- According to the Center for Disease Control and Prevention, the average age of a first-time mother in 2021 was 27 years old. How true does this feel to your school? What might be some challenges to different-age parents in your classrooms?
- What might contribute to Maria feeling as if she does not belong as a parent in this classroom?
- What might the teacher have considered when shaping the orientation to include different experiences and voices?
- How might age present itself as an opportunity in this scenario?

Case 16.5: Someone to Mentor

Kirsten is a mid-level director at the school who has decided to leave at the end of the year for a different school. Her supervisor, Mary, is coordinating the hiring process for Kirsten's replacement, but Kirsten is still heavily involved in recruiting, connecting with candidates, and doing an initial screening. In the third round interview, Kirsten invited two candidates to campus where they met the other mid- and senior-level administrators at the school.

The first candidate, Andrea, has her doctorate in education, a few publications in peer-reviewed journals, and has been recognized as a leader in the professional association for her field. She is smart, well-qualified, and has enough experience to solve most emergencies with ease. Andrea is also known for being very direct, for working from an identity-conscious perspective, and readily calls out issues of race and racism when she sees it. The second candidate, Lilian, is new to the field although she has served in some assistant-level administrator positions at her current school. She is eager to learn, expresses interest in moving up in leadership opportunities, and has enough experience to handle the role but has room to grow. In her interview, Lilian emphasized that she prioritized relationship building, but one of the challenges she is trying to overcome is always being a people pleaser.

When Kirsten and her supervisor were discussing the two candidates after the interview day, Kirsten was sure her supervisor would choose Andrea given Andrea's performance, background, and experience. Andrea certainly could move the work at the school forward. Kirsten was very surprised when her supervisor said, "I'm going to go with Lilian. Lilian seems like she's ready to be mentored, and I think I could do a good job mentoring her. In fact, she reminds me a lot of myself when I was her age. She's young, she's a go-getter, and she has that youthful energy that I had." Kirsten replied, "But Andrea wouldn't need mentoring. She could jump right into this role, keep the work moving forward, and really lead from day one. She has the experience to really make a difference here." Mary replied, "Well, it doesn't even seem like Andrea liked me very much. She was very direct and even hinted that something I said might have been racist. I don't think that's someone who I want to be around. I'm going with someone I can really mentor and shape."

Identity-Conscious Reflection Questions (to be done on your own and/or in group):

- What issues of identity do you notice in this scenario? What is it about your own identities and experiences that made you notice these issues?
- What identities in this scenario do you feel connected to? What identities in this scenario do you feel disconnected or distanced from?

Identity-Conscious Framework (to be discussed as a group)

- Name it: What are the problems or challenges in this scenario that are impacted by identity?
- Own it: Where do these problems or challenges come from? What are the possible reasons that these issues related to identity are emerging?
- Interrupt it: Centering the experiences of identity, what could occur to address barriers, worries, fears, or hesitations in this scenario? What steps could be taken to remedy the issues?
- Take responsibility: What is the follow up to this situation? What might have occurred differently if the people in the scenario were centering identity-consciousness?

Identity-Conscious Discussion Questions (to be discussed as a group)

- What did you notice about your group's process in talking about this case study? How might the identity of your group inform and impact your approach to this case study?

Key Points to Consider
- How, if at all, does Mary's identity and experiences inform and impact this case?
- In hiring processes, how important is it to address qualifications vs personality?
- What values do you believe Mary is expressing when she chooses Lilian over Andrea?
- What might Kirsten's role be in this case?
- What do you make of Mary noting that Andrea mentioned aspects of racism during the interview?

17

Conclusion

> **Chapter at a Glance**
>
> This chapter encourages the reader to be reflective about the process of using an identity-conscious framework in action.

As you worked your way through this book, what did you notice about yourself? What did you notice about others? How did you feel? Why did you feel that way? Where did you experience barriers to understanding? When did you feel confident in your approach?

As teachers and school leaders, we are often caught in the day-to-day rush of confronting problems and quickly solving them. While many situations in our school day require us to respond immediately, there are also many decisions that require us to be thoughtful, introspective, and to slow down our response. It is in the slowing down that we can examine issues of identity, inclusion, and equity. Whenever we rush to respond, we almost always risk leaving other identities and perspectives out of the solutions. Building the habits and skills for an identity-conscious practice means that we can get better at incorporating different perspectives, experiences, and insight into our decision-making.

While you may have gone through the case studies in this book once, I encourage you to revisit them at different points in your life, your career, and your experience. An identity-conscious practice reminds us that what we know and what we pay attention to can change and shift. By revisiting these case studies, and by engaging in dialogue with different groups of people, we may notice that different solutions present themselves each time. This is the foundation of the practice – the openness to adjust, change, shift, adapt and reflect upon the impact of identity.

Thank you for not only building the skills for this work by using the tools in this book, but also for building the habits of learning, reflecting, and moving to action.

References

Bishop, R. S. (1990, March). Windows and mirrors: Children's books and parallel cultures. In *California State University reading conference: 14th annual conference proceedings* (pp. 3–12).

Cherry, K. (2024, January 9). *How attentional bias influences the decisions we make*. What is attentional bias? https://www.verywellmind.com/what-is-an-attentional-bias-2795027

Hailey, S. E., & Olson, K. R. (2013). A social psychologist's guide to the development of racial attitudes. *Social and Personality Psychology Compass, 7*(7), 457–469.

Myers, D., & DeWall, N. (2015). *Psychology*. Worth Publishers.

Patrick, K., Onyeka-Crawford, A., & Duchesneau, N. (rep.). (n.d.). *How to create better and safer learning environments for girls of color*. National Women's Law Center and Ed Trust.

Talusan, L. A. (2022). *Identity-Conscious educator: Building habits and skills for a more inclusive school*. Solution Tree Press.

For Product Safety Concerns and Information please contact our EU representative GPSR@taylorandfrancis.com
Taylor & Francis Verlag GmbH, Kaufingerstraße 24, 80331 München, Germany

www.ingramcontent.com/pod-product-compliance
Lightning Source LLC
Chambersburg PA
CBHW080838230426
43665CB00021B/2885